Teacher's Manual

ACADEMIC *Listening* ENCOUNTERS

AMERICAN STUDIES

Listening
Note Taking
Discussion

Kim Sanabria &
Carlos Sanabria

Intermediate

CAMBRIDGE
UNIVERSITY PRESS

CAMBRIDGE UNIVERSITY PRESS
Cambridge, New York, Melbourne, Madrid, Cape Town, Singapore, São Paulo, Delhi

Cambridge University Press
32 Avenue of the Americas, New York, NY 10013-2473, USA

www.cambridge.org
Information on this title: www.cambridge.org/9780521684347

First published 2008

Printed in the United States of America

A catalog record for this book is available from the British Library

ISBN 978-0-521-68434-7 paperback

Cover and book design: Adventure House, NYC
Text composition: Page Designs International

ACADEMIC ENCOUNTERS

The *Academic Encounters* series uses a sustained content approach to teach students the skills they need to be successful in academic courses. There are two books in the series for each content focus: an *Academic Encounters* title and an *Academic Listening Encounters* title. Please consult your catalog or contact your local sales representative for a current list of available titles.

Titles in the *Academic Encounters* series at publication:

Content Focus and Level	Components	*Academic Encounters*	*Academic Listening Encounters*
HUMAN BEHAVIOR High Intermediate to Low Advanced	Student's Book Teacher's Manual Class Audio Cassettes Class Audio CDs	ISBN 978-0-521-47658-4 ISBN 978-0-521-47660-7	ISBN 978-0-521-60620-2 ISBN 978-0-521-57820-2 ISBN 978-0-521-57819-6 ISBN 978-0-521-78357-6
LIFE IN SOCIETY Intermediate to High Intermediate	Student's Book Teacher's Manual Class Audio Cassettes Class Audio CDs	ISBN 978-0-521-66616-9 ISBN 978-0-521-66613-8	ISBN 978-0-521-75483-5 ISBN 978-0-521-75484-2 ISBN 978-0-521-75485-9 ISBN 978-0-521-75486-6
AMERICAN STUDIES Intermediate	Student's Book Teacher's Manual Class Audio CDs	ISBN 978-0-521-67369-3 ISBN 978-0-521-67370-9	ISBN 978-0-521-68432-3 ISBN 978-0-521-68434-7 ISBN 978-0-521-68433-0

2-Book Sets are available at a discounted price. Each set includes one copy of the Student's Reading Book and one copy of the Student's Listening Book.

Academic Encounters:
Human Behavior 2-Book Set
ISBN 978-0-521-89165-3

Academic Encounters:
Life in Society 2-Book Set
ISBN 978-0-521-54670-6

Academic Encounters:
American Studies 2-Book Set
ISBN 978-0-521-71013-8

Contents

Introduction

This introduction provides a brief overview of *Academic Listening Encounters: American Studies* and a description of the *Academic Encounters* series. It also includes general teaching suggestions and guidelines for all *Academic Listening Encounters* books.

ABOUT *ACADEMIC LISTENING ENCOUNTERS: AMERICAN STUDIES*

Academic Listening Encounters: American Studies is a listening, note-taking, and discussion text based on content taught in American history and culture courses in high schools, colleges, and universities in the United States.*

Correlation with Standards

Academic Listening Encounters: American Studies introduces students to many of the topics and skills in the United States secondary school standards for American history and social studies. For more information about the standards, go to www.cambridge.org/us/esl/academicencounters

TOEFL® iBT Skills

Many of the tasks in *Academic Listening Encounters: American Studies* (as well as those in all *Academic Encounters* books) teach academic skills tested on the TOEFL® iBT test. For a complete list of the tasks, see the Task Index on page 163 of the Student's Book.

THE *ACADEMIC ENCOUNTERS* SERIES

This content-based series is for students who need to improve their academic skills for further study. The series consists of *Academic Encounters* books that help students improve their reading, study skills, and writing; and *Academic Listening Encounters* books that concentrate on listening, note-taking, and discussion skills. Each reading book corresponds in theme to a listening book, and each pair of theme-linked books focuses on a subject commonly taught in academic courses.

For example, *Academic Encounters: American Studies* and *Academic Listening Encounters: American Studies* focus on topics in American history and culture. *Academic Encounters: Life in Society* and *Academic Listening Encounters: Life in Society* focus on sociology; and *Academic Encounters: Human Behavior* and *Academic Listening Encounters: Human Behavior* focus on psychology and human communications. A reading book and a

---

* Note that although the term *Americas* can be used to refer to all of North and South America, *America* is often used to refer to the United States of America alone. The phrase "American Studies" in the title of this book reflects that usage. "American Studies" is an academic discipline with a focus similar to that of this book: United States history and culture.

listening book with the same content focus may be used together to teach a complete four-skills course in English for Academic Purposes.

ACADEMIC LISTENING ENCOUNTERS LISTENING, NOTE-TAKING, AND DISCUSSION BOOKS

The approach

Focusing on a particular academic discipline allows students to gain a sustained experience with one field and encounter concepts and terminology that overlap and grow more complex. It provides students with a realistic sense of taking an academic course. As language and concepts recur and as their skills develop, students gain confidence in their ability to participate in academic pursuits.

The format

Each *Academic Listening Encounters* book consists of five units on different aspects of the discipline. Units are divided into two chapters. Each chapter has four sections and includes an introductory listening exercise, a selection of informal interviews, an opportunity for students to work on and present a topic-related project, and a two-part academic lecture. A variety of listening, note-taking, and discussion tasks accompany the listening material. Chapters are structured to maximize students' comprehension of the chapter topic. Vocabulary and ideas are recycled through the four sections of each chapter and recur in later chapters, as students move from listening to discussion, and from informal to academic discourse.

A chapter-by-chapter Plan of the Book appears in the front of the Student's Book and an alphabetized Task Index is at the back of the Student's Book.

The audio program

The center of *Academic Listening Encounters: Life in Society* is its authentic listening material. The audio program for each chapter includes a warm-up listening exercise designed to introduce the topic, informal interviews that explore a particular aspect of the chapter topic, and a two-part academic lecture on another aspect of the topic. Each of these three types of listening experience exposes students to a different style of discourse, while recycling vocabulary and concepts.

Tasks that are designed to practice a listening skill and involve listening to the audio material (for example, *Listening for Specific Information*, *Listening for Opinions*, or *Note Taking: Listening for Organizational Phrases*), have an earphones icon ⌒ next to the title. This symbol indicates that there is material in the audio program related to the task. A second symbol ▶ PLAY indicates the exact point within the task when the audio material should be played. The complete audio program, which contains the recorded material for the listening and note-taking tasks, is available on audio CDs. The listening script of the complete audio program is in the third section of this Teacher's Manual; it may also be found at the

Academic Encounters section of the Cambridge Web site, www.cambridge. org/esl

An audio CD of the academic lectures, which are an important part of the audio program, is included in the back of each Student's Book to provide students with additional listening practice.

The skills

The three main skills developed in *Academic Listening Encounters* books are listening, note taking, and discussion. Listening is a critical area because unlike text on a page, spoken words are difficult to review. In addition to the content and vocabulary of what they hear, students are challenged by different accents, speeds of delivery, and other features of oral discourse. Tasks in the *Academic Listening Encounters* books guide students in techniques for improving their listening comprehension. These tasks also develop note-taking skills in a structured format that teaches students to write down what they hear in ways that will make it easier to retrieve the information. After the listening and note-taking practice comes an invitation to discussion. Students discuss what they have heard, voice their opinions, compare their experiences, and articulate and exchange viewpoints with other class members, thus making the material their own. Additionally, each chapter gives students the opportunity to work on a project related to the topic, such as conducting a survey or undertaking research, and teaches them the skills necessary to present their findings.

Task commentary boxes

Whenever a task type occurs for the first time in the book, it is headed by a colored commentary box that explains what skill is being practiced and why it is important. When the task occurs again later in the book, it may be accompanied by another commentary box, either as a reminder or to present new information about the skill. At the back of the book, there is an alphabetized index of all the tasks. Page references in boldface indicate tasks that are headed by commentary boxes.

Opportunities for student interaction

Many of the tasks in *Academic Listening Encounters* are divided into steps. Some of these steps are to be done by the student working alone, others by students in pairs or in small groups, and still others by the teacher with the whole class. To make the book as lively as possible, student interaction has been built into most activities. Thus, although the books focus on listening and note-taking skills, discussion is fundamental to each chapter. Students often work collaboratively and frequently compare answers in pairs or small groups.

Order of units

The units do not have to be taught in the order in which they appear in the book, although this order is recommended. To a certain extent, tasks do increase in complexity so that, for example, a note-taking task later in the book may draw upon information that has been included in an earlier unit. Teachers who want to use the material out of order may, however, consult the Plan of the Book at the front of the book or the Task Index at the back of the book to see what information has been presented in earlier units.

Course length

Each chapter of a listening, note-taking, and discussion book is divided into four sections and represents approximately 7–11 hours of classroom material. Thus, with a 90-minute daily class, a teacher could complete all ten chapters in a ten-week course. For use with a shorter course, a teacher could omit chapters or activities within chapters. The material could also be expanded with the use of guest speakers, debates, movies, and other authentic recorded material (see Additional Ideas at the end of each unit in this manual).

CHAPTER FORMAT

1 Getting Started (approximately 1 hour of class time)

This section contains a short reading task and a listening task. The reading is designed to activate students' prior knowledge about the topic, provide them with general concepts and vocabulary, and stimulate their interest. Comprehension and discussion questions elicit their engagement in the topic.

The listening task in this section is determined by the chapter content and involves one of a variety of responses. The task may require students to complete a chart, do a matching exercise, or listen for specific information. The task provides skill-building practice and also gives students listening warm-up on the chapter topic.

2 American Voices (approximately 2–3½ hours of class time)

This section contains informal recorded interviews on issues related to the chapter. It is divided into three subsections:

Before the Interviews (approximately ½ hour)

This subsection contains a prelistening task that calls on students to predict the content of the interview or share what they already know about the topic from their personal experience. Take enough time with this task for all students to contribute. The more they invest in the topic at this point, the more they will get out of the interviews.

Interviews (approximately 1–2 hours)

In this subsection, students listen to interviews related to the topic of the chapter. In most chapters the interviewees are native speakers of English, but voices of immigrants to the United States also enrich the discussions. The interviewees are of different ages and ethnic and social backgrounds, allowing students to gain exposure to the rich and diverse reality of speakers of English. The interviews are divided into two parts to facilitate comprehension: each part can include from one to three interviewees.

Each interview segment begins with a boxed vocabulary preview that glosses words and phrases students may not know. The vocabulary is given in the context in which students will hear it. Reading this vocabulary aloud and exploring its meaning within the context will facilitate students' comprehension.

After each vocabulary preview, students are given the opportunity to scan the upcoming task. Then they listen to the interview and go on to complete the particular task, which might include listening for main ideas or details, drawing inferences, or taking notes on the material in order to retell what they have heard. This approach provides a framework for listening, teaches basic listening skills, and allows students to demonstrate their understanding of the interviews.

After the Interviews (approximately ½–1 hour)
In this subsection, students explore the topic more deeply through examining graphic material related to the content of the interviews, thinking critically about what they have heard, or sharing their perspective. Most of the tasks in this section are for pairs or small groups and allow for informal feedback from every student.

3 In Your Own Voice (approximately 1½–2½ hours of class time)

This section continues to build on the chapter topic and is designed to give students the opportunity to take creative control of the topic at hand. Specific tasks are determined by the chapter content. They may include:

- *Personalizing the content*, in which students talk with partners or in small groups, sharing their experiences and supporting their points of view
- *Gathering data*, in which students conduct surveys or interviews of classmates or people outside the class, or in which they undertake small research projects
- *Presenting data*, in which students organize their data and present it individually or in small groups
- *Responding to presentations*, in which students discuss the content of presentations and analyze the effectiveness of a presenter's style

4 Academic Listening and Note Taking (approximately 2½–4 hours of class time)

This section contains a formal, recorded, academic lecture related to the topic of the chapter. It is divided into three subsections:

Before the Lecture (1–1½ hours)
The first task of this subsection asks students to predict the content of the lecture, explore what they already know about the topic, or build their background knowledge and vocabulary by doing a task related to a brief reading, syllabus, or other written entry. As with *Before the Interviews*, this section promotes the student's investment in the topic.

Each chapter then proceeds to an academic note-taking skill, determined by the language of the lecture itself and sequenced to build upon skills studied in previous chapters. The skill is explained in a task commentary box, and the listening task is designed to practice it. The recorded material used for the task is drawn from the lecture.

Lecture (1–1½ hours)

In this subsection, students hear the lecture itself. To facilitate comprehension, all lectures are divided into two parts.

Each lecture part begins with a matching or multiple-choice vocabulary task to prepare students for the language they will encounter in the lecture and help them develop their ability to guess meaning from context. Potentially unfamiliar words and phrases are given in the context in which they will be used in the lecture. Reading the items aloud, studying their pronunciation, and exploring their use and meaning will prepare students for hearing them in the lecture.

Following the vocabulary task, students preview a comprehension task designed to provide a framework for their listening and note taking. The task may involve completing a summary or outline, or answering comprehension questions. The task may recycle the note-taking skill taught before the lecture or add a related skill. Students are instructed to take notes during each part of the lecture and then use their notes to complete the lecture comprehension task. Previewing the task will enable students to answer the questions in a more confident and focused manner.

After the Lecture (½–1 hour)

This subsection invites students to share their perspective through discussion questions that allow them to analyze the chapter content more critically. It may also present additional information or ask students to apply what they have learned.

GENERAL TEACHING SUGGESTIONS

Section Introductions

Each chapter in the Student's Book is divided into four sections. Each section begins with a brief preview: *In this section you will . . .* Always read these previews together with the class and answer any questions that arise. Take enough time with this task for all students to contribute.

Tasks and Commentary Boxes

Virtually every activity throughout *Academic Listening Encounters* is presented as a task. Each task practices a specific language or thinking skill critical for academic-bound students. Most tasks are recycled throughout the book. (See the Plan of the Book in the front of the Student's Book or the Task Index at the back of the Student's Book.) The first time a task title appears, it is followed by a shaded task commentary box containing information about the task. Always read this commentary and check for understanding. Ask students: *What are we doing in this exercise? Why is this useful?*

Listening Tasks

Before students listen to the recorded material and complete the task, make sure that they read over the task and think about what information they will need to listen for.

Replay audio excerpts as many times as you think will benefit the majority of students and enable them to complete tasks successfully, including the interviews and lectures. Students are not expected to catch every word; it is not necessary.

As an alternative to the recording, you may try reading the lectures to your students. (See the section titled Listening Script in this Teacher's Manual.) Try to incorporate appropriate stress, intonation, and body language.

In Your Own Voice

In Your Own Voice (Section 3 of each chapter in the Student's Book) usually concludes with students giving oral presentations about a project they have completed. Keep students on task by having them respond to the presentations. They can take notes, ask questions, make comments, and suggest possible ways presenters could improve their style. You may also want to give a content quiz on the presentations. One way to do this is to use your own notes to write one general question about each presentation. Then dictate your questions and allow students to refer to their notes in order to respond.

Photos, Cartoons, and Drawings

All of the art in the Student's Book is intended to build interest and comprehension. In many cases, students are directed to think about the art as part of a task. In cases where they are not specifically asked to do this – such as the art at the beginning of units and chapters – be sure to draw their attention to the art and discuss its connection to the topic.

Vocabulary

Unfamiliar vocabulary is a stumbling block to comprehension, so a great effort has been made to gloss or preteach most of the language that is unfamiliar to students. In each part of Section 2 (American Voices), have students read the vocabulary and glosses in the box by themselves first; then read the vocabulary items aloud so that students can hear how the words are pronounced. Check for understanding of glosses given in the vocabulary boxes.

Each part of the lecture in Section 4 (Academic Listening and Note Taking) begins with a task called Guessing Vocabulary from Context. Begin by reading the vocabulary aloud. When checking the vocabulary task, give the correct answers yourself only as a last resort.

Any photos or realia that you can bring to class will help with comprehension and retention of vocabulary.

Comprehension and Discussion Questions

One of the goals of *Academic Listening Encounters* is to develop oral fluency, and for this reason there is a great deal of pair and small group work. If students have communicated successfully in pairs or small groups, they will feel more confident about sharing with the class. Let students control the all-class comprehension checks or discussions whenever possible. They can divide up the questions, assigning each one to a different student or pair of students working together. Use the board, and ask for a student volunteer to do the writing. For opinion questions, stress that there are no right or wrong answers. Encourage students to give their own ideas, and model acceptance of all opinions. For comprehension questions – as with vocabulary – give the answers yourself only as a last resort.

Give students plenty of time for discussion questions; circulate and encourage all students to voice their opinions. Whenever possible, pair and group students from different cultures. Move on to the next activity before discussion begins to die out or digress from the subject at hand.

Teacher's Role

As much as you can, try to take part as an equal in discussions and activities. Because many of the tasks in *Academic Listening Encounters* books are based on students' own knowledge and opinions, you should spend most of your time in the role of a participant or facilitator rather than authority figure. You will probably discover that the students are teaching you as much as you are teaching them.

Homework

Some of the activities in *Academic Listening Encounters* books can be done at home. For example, students can read and then think or write about given discussion questions, and they can do the Guessing Vocabulary from Context task before the lecture. They can also do many of the After the Lecture tasks at home, using the notes they took while listening to the lecture. Interviews, research, and surveys are normally done outside of class time.

Encourage students to gain additional listening practice by listening at home to the chapter lectures that are on the audio CD in the back of the Student's Book. Depending on the level of the class, you may want students to listen either before or after you have played the lecture for them in class. If you think it will be helpful for students, you can also let them know that the listening script for the complete audio program is available at the *Academic Encounters* section of the Cambridge Web site, www.cambridge.org/esl

Testing

The lecture in each chapter may be used as a listening and note-taking test. Quizzes on the content of the lectures are in the Lecture Quizzes section of this manual and may be photocopied for distribution to the students. Students may answer each quiz either on the quiz sheet or on their own paper. When taking the tests, students should refer only to the notes they took for the lecture tasks. Answers to the quizzes are in the last section of this manual, Lecture Quiz Answers.

Chapter-by-Chapter Teaching Suggestions and Answer Key

Unit

Laws of the Land

Unit Title Page (Student's Book page 1)

Read the title of the unit aloud and elicit from students why a country needs laws and what areas of life a country's laws affect. Have students look at the photograph and discuss its relationship to the unit title.

Read the unit summary paragraph with students. Introduce them to some of the key words that will be used in the unit: *Constitution*, *structure*, *background*, *vote*, and *amendments*. Chapter 1 discusses the basic organization of the U.S. government and the history behind it. Chapter 2 is about the Bill of Rights and controversies around the First Amendment.

Because this is the first unit in the book, review the structure of the chapters. Explain that in each chapter students will learn new information and practice their listening skills by listening to interviews and a lecture. Other tasks will help them to refine their note-taking skills. There are many opportunities to discuss the issues presented with classmates. In Section 3, In Your Own Voice, students will also have the opportunity to participate in an individual, group, or class project related to the topic of the chapter.

Chapter 1

The Foundations of Government

Look at the picture and discuss its relationship to the chapter title and the chapter description on the unit title page.

1 GETTING STARTED (Student's Book pages 2–3)

READING AND THINKING ABOUT THE TOPIC

This short passage introduces several important facts about the U.S. government: It is a *republic* and a *democracy* and guided by the principle of *federalism*. The paragraph also introduces the three branches of government and explains the purpose of the system of *checks and balances*. These terms will probably require some amplification.

Answers to step 2 (Student's Book page 3)

1 Three principles that form the foundation of the United States government are: it is a republic, it is a democracy, and it is based on the principle of federalism.

2 Citizens of the United States have the right to vote in free elections.

3 The purpose of the system of checks and balances is to make sure none of the three branches of government has too much power.

⌒ PREVIEWING THE TOPIC

Answers to step 2 (Student's Book page 3)

  _3_   **a** The national symbol of the United States

  _5_   **b** The 13 original states of the United States

  _1_   **c** The fact that America is a country with a strong foundation

  _4_   **d** The fact that the United States is one nation made of many states and many people

  _2_   **e** The year that the United States became independent from Britain

2   AMERICAN VOICES: Manuel, Mary, Kelly, Ralph, and Bob

(Student's Book pages 4–9)

BEFORE THE INTERVIEWS

BUILDING BACKGROUND KNOWLEDGE AND VOCABULARY

Look at the picture with students and elicit their reactions. How is this scene similar to or different from their own impression or experience of voting?

Answers to step 2 (Student's Book pages 4–5)

> All U.S. citizens have the right to <u>vote</u> in national <u>elections</u> at the age of 18. Voting is also called "going to <u>the polls</u>." In the United States, voting is voluntary, not <u>compulsory</u>. Voters choose the <u>candidate</u> they support and vote for that person on Election Day.
>
> Voters may make their decision for different reasons. One reason might be that they support one <u>party</u> – for example, Democratic or Republican. Another reason might be that they feel strongly about a particular <u>issue</u> such as education, crime, or foreign policy, and they want to express their opinion by electing the candidate who agrees with them.
>
> Most of the time, there are only two main candidates in U.S. elections – a Democrat and a Republican. Occasionally, a third candidate <u>runs for office</u>, but third-party candidates almost never win in the United States.

EXAMINING GRAPHIC MATERIAL

Answers (Student's Book page 5)

1 The graph shows facts (voter turnout in different years) and trends (the rise and fall in voter turnout).

2 Voter turnout was highest in 1960.

3 Voter turnout dropped between 1960 and 1980.

4 Approximately 55 percent voted in 2004.

5 Answers will vary.

INTERVIEW WITH MANUEL, MARY, KELLY, AND RALPH: Reasons for voting or not voting

Look at the pictures of the interviewees and read aloud the vocabulary in the box on page 6 of the Student's Book.

🎧 LISTENING FOR DIFFERENT WAYS OF SAYING *YES* AND *NO*

Answers to step 2 (Student's Book page 6)

Manuel	No
Mary	Yes
Kelly	Yes
Ralph	No

Answers to step 3 (Student's Book page 7)

b	1
a	2
d	3
c	4

INTERVIEW WITH BOB: Issues that influence voter turnout

Look at Bob's picture and read the vocabulary aloud.

🎧 LISTENING FOR MAIN IDEAS IN AN INTERVIEW

Answers to step 2 (Student's Book page 8)

1 c and e
2 a
3 d, e, and f

AFTER THE INTERVIEWS

RETELLING WHAT YOU HAVE HEARD

Explain to students that retelling is a basic way of checking their understanding and helping them review important ideas. Encourage students to be creative in explaining the interviewees' viewpoints and to use the vocabulary they have learned.

SHARING YOUR OPINION

This task asks students to contribute their opinion to a group discussion. Encourage them to use the expressions from the list and to agree or respectfully disagree with other class members. Encourage students to support their viewpoint with details and examples.

3 IN YOUR OWN VOICE (Student's Book page 10)

SHARING YOUR KNOWLEDGE

The purpose of this task is to allow students to contribute their knowledge to the general body of information that everyone in the class should know. It is also designed to be interactive and engaging. You can establish a time frame of approximately 15 minutes for students to complete the entire game board or organize the questions according to your own class needs. The answers are at the bottom of page 11 of the Student's Book.

4 ACADEMIC LISTENING AND NOTE TAKING: The Structure of the U.S. Federal Government (Student's Book pages 11–15)

BEFORE THE LECTURE

🎧 LISTENING FOR THE PLAN OF A LECTURE

Answers to step 1 (Student's Book page 11)

b	**1**
a	**2**
c	**3**
e	**4**
d	**5**

NOTE TAKING: USING INFORMATION THE LECTURER PUTS ON THE BOARD

Students can photocopy the chart in the Student's Book or draw their own charts in their notebooks.

LECTURE, PART ONE: The Three Branches of the U.S. Federal Government

GUESSING VOCABULARY FROM CONTEXT

Answers to step 2 (Student's Book page 13)

f	**1**
a	**2**
b	**3**
d	**4**
e	**5**
g	**6**
h	**7**
c	**8**

⌒ NOTE TAKING: USING INFORMATION THE LECTURER PUTS ON THE BOARD

Sample answers to step 1 (Student's Book page 14)

Branch of government	Legislative	Executive	Judicial
Name	Congress: – Senate – House of Representatives	*President*	*Supreme Court*
Name of officials	Senators Representatives	*President* *Vice President* *Secretaries*	*Justices*
Responsibilities	makes laws	*approves laws*	*interprets laws*
Details	Senate = 100 members (2 from each state) House = 435 members (number depends on size of state population)	*Many secretaries:* *– Secretary of State* *– Secretary of Defense* *– Secretary of Education* *etc.*	*– 9 justices* *– decide if laws are constitutional*

LECTURE, PART TWO: The System of Checks and Balances

GUESSING VOCABULARY FROM CONTEXT

Answers to step 2 (Student's Book page 14)

a	**1**
d	**2**
e	**3**
c	**4**
b	**5**

⌒ NOTE TAKING: TAKING GOOD LECTURE NOTES

Answers to step 2 (Student's Book page 15)

The System of Checks and Balances

Why is fed. gov. divided into branches?
   Founders wanted to avoid dictatorship. ⎫ *wrote main ideas*
   Invented system of checks & balances. ⎭

                                             wrote only important words
                                             instead of complete sentences
Def: the 3 branches ⟵
   have sep. respons. + ⟵   *used abbreviations*
   have power to check (limit) each other's actions   *and symbols*

Ex:
   1. Selection of Supreme Court Justices
      – Pres. Chooses Justices, but Cong. can disapprove   ⎫ *indented examples*
   2. Cong. passes laws, but Pres. can veto   ⎬ *and details*
   3. Cong. passes law & Pres. signs, but Supreme Court   ⎭
      can say it's unconstitutional

AFTER THE LECTURE

SHARING YOUR KNOWLEDGE

Encourage students to use the information and vocabulary they have learned to describe the pictures on page 15 of the Student's Book.

Chapter 1 Lecture Quiz

See the Lecture Quiz section at the back of this Teacher's Manual for a photocopiable quiz on the lecture for Chapter 1. Quiz answers can be found on page 128.

Chapter 2

Constitutional Issues Today

Look at the picture and discuss its relationship to the chapter title and the chapter description on the unit title page.

1 GETTING STARTED (Student's Book pages 16–18)

READING AND THINKING ABOUT THE TOPIC

This passage gives background information about the signing of the U.S. Constitution and the process of amending the Constitution. In particular, it explains the Bill of Rights and gives details about why interpreting this document presents difficulties. Words that might require explanation are *accuse of*, *controversial*, *censorship*, *offensive*, and *conflict*.

Sample answers to step 2 (Student's Book page 17)

1 In 1786, George Washington, James Madison, Alexander Hamilton, and other leaders met in Philadelphia to talk about how to organize the new government of the United States. The result of their work was the U.S. Constitution.

2 The Bill of Rights is the first 10 amendments added to the Constitution in 1791, which include freedom of speech, freedom of religion, and the right of people accused of crimes to have a lawyer.

3 Censorship and whether or not the government can listen to private telephone conversations are two controversial topics.

⌂ UNDERSTANDING NUMBERS, DATES, AND TIME EXPRESSIONS

Answers to steps 1 and 2 (Student's Book page 18)

July 1, 1971	9. Voting age lowered from 21 to 18
1920	8. Women given right to vote
from 1787 to 1920	7. Only men had right to vote
1870	6. African-American men given right to vote
1865	5. Slavery ended
between 1861 and 1865	4. American Civil War
1791	3. Bill of Rights became part of U.S. Constitution
1789	2. Constitution adopted
July 4, 1776	1. United States declared independence from Britain

2 AMERICAN VOICES: Magda, Hang, and Gloria
(Student's Book pages 19–23)

BEFORE THE INTERVIEWS

PREVIEWING THE TOPIC

Answers to step 2 (Student's Book page 19)
a First
b Sixth
c Second
d Fourth
e First
f First
g First
h Fifth
i First

INTERVIEW WITH MAGDA AND HANG: Important constitutional rights

Look at the photographs of Magda and Hang and read the vocabulary in the box on page 20 aloud with the class.

🎧 LISTENING FOR SPECIFIC INFORMATION

Answers to step 2 (Student's Book page 21)

1 b
2 a
3 a
4 a
5 a
6 a
7 b

INTERVIEW WITH GLORIA: Another important right

Look at the picture of Gloria and read the vocabulary in the box on page 22 aloud with the class.

🎧 LISTENING FOR SPECIFIC INFORMATION

Answers to step 2 (Student's Book page 22)

> Gloria focuses on the right to (1) bear arms. She believes the (2) Second Amendment gives American citizens this right. Gloria says there are (3) two groups of people who own guns. One group is (4) criminals, and they will own guns whether it is (5) legal or not. The second group is (6) responsible people who own guns for (7) good reasons, for example, for (8) sports or for (9) self-protection. Gloria explains that the (10) police can't be everywhere, so some people might feel that they (11) need a gun to protect themselves.

AFTER THE INTERVIEWS

UNDERSTANDING HUMOR ABOUT THE TOPIC

Remind students about the right to freedom of expression and elicit their reactions to the cartoon. Allow them to compare their reactions with other students' reactions.

Sample answers to step 2 (Student's Book page 23)

1 The speakers are at a party having a casual conversation.

2 He means that the Constitution covers different rights.

3 No, the speaker is exaggerating.

4 The speaker is not serious. He is making a joke by oversimplifying the meaning of the Constitution.

5 Answers will vary.

3 **IN YOUR OWN VOICE** (Student's Book page 24)

ROLE PLAYING

Make sure students understand that role playing is a valuable way to review information, practice new vocabulary, and develop communication skills. Encourage students to exercise their creative talents and negotiate solutions with their classmates.

4 **ACADEMIC LISTENING AND NOTE TAKING: The First Amendment** (Student's Book pages 25–32)

BEFORE THE LECTURE

PREDICTING WHAT YOU WILL HEAR

Point out to students that over time, the concept of freedom of speech has become broadened to all types of expression, for example, in writing and art. The terms *freedom of speech* and *freedom of expression* are often used interchangeably.

Sample answers to step 2, item 1 (Student's Book page 25)

1 People are exercising their right to assembly and to freedom of speech.

2 Parents say they have a right to contact their children if they need to, exercising their freedom of speech.

3 The author and the library are both exercising freedom of speech.

4 The artist and the newspaper are exercising freedom of speech, even though the cartoon may offend other people's religious beliefs.

5 The police officer is trying to exercise his right to freedom of religion.

🎧 NOTE TAKING: LISTENING FOR MAIN IDEAS AND SUPPORTING DETAILS

Answers to steps 1 and 2 (Student's Book pages 26–27)

Excerpt 1

 _4_ For instance, an employer can't hire or fire you just because he likes or doesn't like your religion.

 _1_ What does it mean to have freedom of religion?

 _6_ What I mean is that Americans are free to wear any kind of religious clothing they prefer.

 _3_ Now this freedom affects Americans in many ways.

 _2_ Basically it means two things: First, Americans are free to practice their religion without interference from the government, and second, there is no national religion.

 _5_ And freedom of religion even includes how you dress.

Excerpt 2

 _6_ In fact, the courts have said that freedom of speech includes all forms of expression, meaning words, pictures, music, even the way you wear your hair!

 _4_ You're also free to read or listen to other people's ideas.

___1___ The next freedom listed in the First Amendment is maybe the most famous one, because it's the one that all of us practice every single day, and that's freedom of speech.

___5___ But in addition, freedom of speech includes what we call "symbolic speech" – like wearing the clothes you like.

___3___ Basically, it means you are free to talk openly about your ideas, even if other people disagree with them.

___2___ What does that mean, exactly?

LECTURE, PART ONE: Overview of the First Amendment

GUESSING VOCABULARY FROM CONTEXT

Answers to step 2 (Student's Book page 27)

b	1
i	2
f	3
c	4
d	5
j	6
h	7
a	8
e	9
g	10

NOTE TAKING: USING SYMBOLS AND ABBREVIATIONS

Answers to step 3 (Student's Book page 28–29)

1st amend = 5 f'doms

1. F'dom of relig
   = Amers. can practice their relig w/o interference from gov't
   U.S. has no national relig

2. F'dom of spch
   = f'dom to talk openly about ideas
   Inc. "symbolic speech" – inc clothes +/& all forms of exp, e.g., words, pictures, etc.

3. F'dom of the press
   = f'dom to publish diff ideas & opinions
   Inc. books, newspaper, magazines, Internet
       e.g./ex., cartoon making joke about pres
       journalist can write article criticizing the gov't

4. F'dom of assembly
   = can meet in grps
   E.g./ex., college sts demonstrate

5. F'dom of petition
   = citizens have f'dom to ask gov't to change things

To sum: we use the term f'dom of exp to talk about all 5 f'doms.

LECTURE, PART TWO: *First Amendment Controversies*

GUESSING VOCABULARY FROM CONTEXT

Answers to step 2 (Student's Book page 30)

c	**1**
d	**2**
e	**3**
a	**4**
b	**5**
f	**6**

🎧 NOTE TAKING: USING A MAP TO ORGANIZE YOUR NOTES

Answers to step 1 (Student's Book page 30)

This part of the lecture is about the limits of free speech.

Two examples are given: flag burning and cell phone use.

No and *yes* signify opposing opinions about these controversies.

Information missing is:

YES:

1st amend. guarantees f'dom of exp

NO:

Cell phones make noise in class

Answers to steps 2 and 3 (Student's Book page 31)

Main idea: What does freedom of religion mean in practice?

Example: Should children be allowed to pray in public schools?

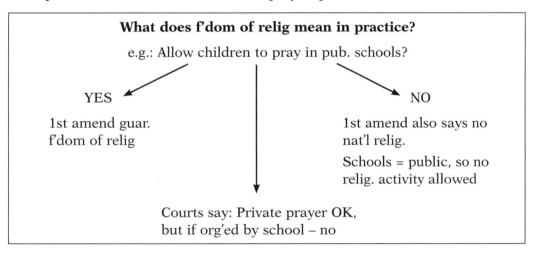

What does f'dom of relig mean in practice?

e.g.: Allow children to pray in pub. schools?

YES

1st amend guar. f'dom of relig

NO

1st amend also says no nat'l relig.

Schools = public, so no relig. activity allowed

Courts say: Private prayer OK, but if org'ed by school – no

AFTER THE LECTURE

CONDUCTING A SURVEY

Explain the benefits of surveys to the class: they allow practice of key information and vocabulary; they put students in real-life situations; they sometimes bring unexpected results.

If possible, allow plenty of time for students to complete their surveys outside of class and to fully explain their experience to other class members.

Chapter 2 Lecture Quiz

See the Lecture Quiz section at the back of this Teacher's Manual for a photocopiable quiz on the lecture for Chapter 2. Quiz answers can be found on page 128.

Additional Ideas for Unit 1

Key topics in this unit include the U.S. Constitution, the structure and history of the U.S. government, the three branches of government, the Bill of Rights, and controversies surrounding the First Amendment.

1 Have students look at the U.S. Constitution, either in a library or online, and identify the amendments that have been added over time. Students can also list the amendments and the dates they were passed. Have students discuss which amendments they think are particularly important and why.

2 Have students search for newspaper articles that involve freedom of speech issues or bring some to class. Discuss the articles in class or ask students to present short summaries of the articles to each other or in small groups.

3 Have students borrow a book on the history of the United States or look for an overview online and familiarize themselves with key events in the country's history. One way to do this is to divide the class into groups and have each group research a different period of the country's history.

4 Ask students to research government symbols found on the U.S. flag and paper money.

5 Have students identify some of the Founding Fathers and prepare a short biography of their lives, including information such as when they were born and what they are most famous for.

A Diverse Nation

Unit Title Page (Student's Book page 33)

Read the title of the unit aloud and discuss the meaning of the word *diverse*. Then read the paragraph aloud and clarify the two time periods that students will be studying in this unit. Chapter 3 focuses on the wave of immigration that lasted from the mid-nineteenth century to the early twentieth century and deals mostly with immigrants from Europe. Chapter 4 discusses the wave of immigration that began during the second half of the twentieth century and continues today, and it focuses on immigrants from all over the world.

Look at the photograph and discuss its significance. Also, make sure students understand the following terms: *wave, prejudice, contributions,* and *countries and cultures of origin*.

Chapter 3

The Origins of Diversity

Look at the picture and discuss its relationship to the chapter title and the chapter description on the unit title page.

1 GETTING STARTED (Student's Book pages 34–36)

READING AND THINKING ABOUT THE TOPIC

This short passage provides the context within which the first big wave of immigration took place. Make sure students can identify the appropriate time periods, immigrant groups, and reasons for immigration to the United States. They might also need help with the following vocabulary: *ethnic*, *settlers*, *slaves*, *tribes*, and *left their mark on*.

> **Answers to step 2** (Student's Book page 35)
> 1 The United States is considered a country of immigrants because its people come from a variety of religious, economic, racial, and ethnic backgrounds.
> 2 The largest groups to come to the United States between 1820 and 1930 were the Germans, Irish, Italians, and Jews.

BUILDING BACKGROUND KNOWLEDGE

↑	There was not enough food in parts of Europe in the 1820s.
↑	Beginning in the 1880s, steamships made it faster and easier to cross the Atlantic Ocean.
↑	During the 1880s, there was violence against Jews in Russia.
↑	World War I began in Europe in 1914.
↓	The United States entered the war in 1917.
↓	In the 1920s, there were important changes in U.S. laws that limited immigration.
↓	In 1929, the American stock market "crashed." This was the beginning of the effects of the Great Depression in the United States. Millions of Americans lost their money and their jobs, and it was almost impossible to find work.

⌒ LISTENING FOR NUMERICAL INFORMATION

Answer to step 2 (Student's Book page 36)

Graph 2 is the correct version.

2 AMERICAN VOICES: Patrick, Eunice, and John

(Student's Book pages 37–40)

BEFORE THE INTERVIEWS

BUILDING BACKGROUND KNOWLEDGE

Answers to step 2 (Student's Book page 37)

Push	Pull			
	a	1	My great-grandparents came from Italy around 1890. There were more jobs in the United States.	
c		2	Many people in my grandparents' village in Russia were attacked because of their religious beliefs.	
	d	3	My mother came over to the States to meet up with my father. They were in love and planned to get married.	
a		4	My parents came from a farming village in Greece. But there wasn't enough land there for people to farm.	
a		5	In 1848, there was a potato famine in Ireland. All the potato plants died, and there was very little food for years after that.	
	b	6	The United States was a democracy. We could vote for whoever we wanted to.	
b		7	In the village we came from, it was dangerous to express your real opinions.	

EXAMINING GRAPHIC MATERIAL

Answers to step 2 (Student's Book page 38)

1 From 1840 to1860, most immigrants came from [northern and western Europe / the Americas / Asia / eastern and southern Europe / other places].

2 Most immigrants from eastern and southern Europe came to the United States in the period [1840–1860 / 1880–1900].

3 From 1840 to 1900, the percentage of immigrants from the Americas [rose a little / stayed exactly the same / fell quickly].

4 The percentage of immigrants from Asia [increased a lot / stayed about the same / fell sharply] during the 1840–1900 time period.

INTERVIEW WITH PATRICK: Immigration to the United States in the 1860s

Look at the photograph of Patrick on page 39 and read the vocabulary in the box on page 38 aloud.

ANSWERING TRUE/FALSE QUESTIONS

Review the directions with students and clarify that if part of a statement is false, then the entire statement is false.

Answers to step 2 (Student's Book page 39)

F	1	Patrick's grandparents came from the same village in Ireland.
F	2	Patrick's family came to the United States for economic reasons.
F	3	The whole family came.
T	4	
T	5	
T	6	
F	7	Many Irish immigrants worked in factories, in the police force, and as firefighters.
F	8	Patrick comes from a large family.

INTERVIEW WITH EUNICE AND JOHN: Immigration to the United States in the 1900s

Look at the photographs of Eunice and John on page 40 and read the vocabulary in the box on page 39 aloud.

LISTENING FOR SPECIFIC INFORMATION

Remind students that previewing the chart will help students identify the information they must listen for.

Answers to step 2 (Student's Book page 40)

	Eunice	**John**
Ethnic or religious background	*Jewish*	*Italian*
Country their relatives came from	*Russia*	*Italy*
Reasons their relatives came to the United States	*Religious: there was a fear of religious persecution* *Political: you couldn't criticize the government* *Economic: the chance to have better jobs and live more comfortably*	*Economic: the economy was bad, and they couldn't make a living.*
Experience of their family in America	*Difficult, because they were very poor. It was also hard to keep the family close.*	*The trip was hard. They didn't have money when they arrived and didn't speak the language. It was also difficult during the Depression.*

AFTER THE INTERVIEWS

RETELLING WHAT YOU HAVE HEARD (Student's Book page 40)

As a class, review the instructions for this activity so that it goes smoothly. Everyone should write a question for each of the interviewees in this chapter (Patrick, Eunice, and John) and then work in groups of three. Each person will get a turn to speak in the role of one of the interviewees and respond to the questions of their classmates.

3 IN YOUR OWN VOICE (Student's Book pages 41–42)

CONDUCTING RESEARCH

Review the instructions and stress the importance of using appropriate sources for research, representing it accurately, and making a note of the source of the information. You may wish to provide students with a simple format for writing down their sources.

APPLYING WHAT YOU HAVE LEARNED

This activity builds squarely on the previous task and asks students to use their imagination and creativity to envisage the lives of the four people who immigrated to the United States: Martin O'Reilly, Salvatore Leo, Katya Prinz, and Maria Karas.

4 ACADEMIC LISTENING AND NOTE TAKING: Immigrants to America Face Prejudice but Make Lasting Contributions

(Student's Book pages 43–49)

BEFORE THE LECTURE

BUILDING BACKGROUND KNOWLEDGE AND VOCABULARY

Make sure students fully understand the vocabulary presented in this exercise, especially: *contributions, prejudice, unskilled, infrastructure, agricultural, widespread,* and *stereotypes*. They will need this vocabulary in order to understand the lecture.

Answers to step 2 (Student's Book page 43)

UNIT 1: Prejudice Toward Immigrant Groups
Readings:
1 Strong Anti-Irish Sentiment Begins to Grow
2 Widespread Anti-Immigrant Feelings
3 Religious Prejudice and Stereotypes

UNIT 2: Contributions of Immigrant Groups
Readings:
1 Many Unskilled Workers Needed for Nation's Infrastructure
2 Jobs in Construction and Services
3 Needs of Agricultural and Industrial Production

⌒ NOTE TAKING: LISTENING FOR TRANSITIONAL PHRASES THAT INTRODUCE SUPPORTING DETAILS

Answers to step 2 (Student's Book page 44)
1 for instance
2 By / I mean / like
3 in fact
4 One reason for this was
5 in other words

LECTURE, PART ONE: Immigrants Face Prejudice

GUESSING VOCABULARY FROM CONTEXT

Answers to step 2 (Student's Book page 45)
a	1
c	2
e	3
b	4
f	5
d	6

🎧 NOTE TAKING: USING TELEGRAPHIC LANGUAGE

Sample answers to step 2 (Student's Book page 46)

Imms Face Prejudice

I.   4 maj imm grps imm'ed to U.S. @ this time:
     Germans, Irish, Jews, Italians

II. Prejudice
     Ex: call imms cruel names, refuse to rent them apt. or give them jobs

III. Reasons for prej
     A. Size of imm pop: 30 mill
     B. Diff relig
        ex: prej vs Catholics + Jews
     C. Diff langs + unfamiliar customs, foods, clothes, etc.
     D. People scared imms would not share democ. values
        ex: prej vs Germans during WWI
     E. Amers. afraid of losing jobs

LECTURE, PART TWO: Immigrants Make Lasting Contributions

GUESSING VOCABULARY FROM CONTEXT

Answers to step 2 (Student's Book page 47)

   e   **1**
   b   **2**
   a   **3**
   f   **4**
   c   **5**
   d   **6**

🎧 NOTE TAKING: ORGANIZING YOUR NOTES IN COLUMNS

Sample answers to step 2 (Student's Book page 48)

Immigrants Make Lasting Contributions

Immigrant Groups	Examples of Contributions
Germans	farmers, tailors, bakers, butchers
Irish	built infrastructure of many Am cities inc. skilled wkrs, e.g., plumbers + unskilled, e.g., factory wkrs
Jews	popular music, entertainment, education, science, clothing industry
Italians	built roads, canals, bridges, buildings, and railroads
All imms	Contrib to ec and culture e.g., langs, food, music, relig, lifestyles

---

AFTER THE LECTURE

ANSWERING MULTIPLE CHOICE QUESTIONS

Some students might not be familiar with paper versions of multiple-choice tests. Review the instructions for "bubbling in" carefully.

Answers to step 1 (Student's Book page 49)
1 b
2 b
3 a
4 b
5 a
6 c

Chapter 3 Lecture Quiz

See the Lecture Quiz section at the back of this Teacher's Manual for a photocopiable quiz on the lecture for Chapter 3. Quiz answers can be found on page 129.

Chapter 4

Diversity in Today's United States

Look at the photograph and discuss its relationship to the chapter title and the chapter description on the unit title page.

1 **GETTING STARTED** (Student's Book pages 50–52)

READING AND THINKING ABOUT THE TOPIC

> This passage describes the change in immigration patterns since 1965 and elaborates on new reasons why immigrants choose to make the United States their home. It also deals with the topic of adaptation. Words that might require attention are *adapt*, *combination*, and *hyphenated*. Students may have a strong reaction to the concept of a *hyphenated American* (such as a Mexican-American or a Chinese-American) and disagree about what it means. This gets to the core of issues about how immigrants adapt to their new culture, so discussion should be encouraged.

Answers to step 2 (Student's Book page 51)

1 A century ago, most immigrants to the United States came from Europe. These days, they come from countries such as Mexico, China, and India, as well as the Caribbean and eastern Europe.

2 Immigrants continue to come for economic and political reasons, but also because of diversity, educational opportunities, and health care.

3 Some come to join their families, while others leave their families behind. Some are poor, and others make a lot of money. Some adapt completely, some maintain a hyphenated identity, and some keep their original culture for their whole lives.

♫ LISTENING FOR PERCENTAGES AND FRACTIONS

Answers to step 2 (Student's Book page 52)

1 The time periods shown are 1901–1940, 1941–1980, and 1981–2000.

2 The parts of the world shown are Europe, Latin America, and Asia.

3 Answers will vary.

Answers to step 3

1901–1940	1941–1980	1981–2000
Europe: 79%	Europe: 34%	Latin America: 47%
Latin America: 6%	Latin America: 34%	Asia: 34%
Asia: 4%	Asia: 19%	Europe: 13%
Other: 11%	Other: 13%	Other: 6%

Answers to step 4

1 The percentage of immigrants from Europe has gone down. The percentage of immigrants from Latin America and Asia has gone up a lot.

2 Between 1981 and 2000, 47% (almost ½ of all immigrants) came from Latin America, and 34% (about ⅓) came from Asia. Only 13% came from Europe.

3 Answers will vary.

2 AMERICAN VOICES: Agustín, Nadezhda, Chao, Alvin, Minsoo, and Abdoul-Aziz (Student's Book pages 53–56)

BEFORE THE INTERVIEWS

SHARING YOUR OPINION

Make sure students fully understand the significance of these factors that affect immigration patterns to the United States. Ask them to share and explain the reasons for their responses.

BUILDING BACKGROUND KNOWLEDGE

Answers to step 2 (Student's Book page 53; answers can also be found on page 59)

b	**1**
c	**2**
d	**3**
e	**4**
f	**5**
g	**6**
a	**7**

INTERVIEW WITH AGUSTIN, NADEZHDA, AND CHAO: Reasons for coming to the United States

Look at the photographs of Agustín, Nadezhda, and Chao and read the vocabulary in the box on page 54 aloud. Have students predict the information that might be included in the interviews.

LISTENING FOR SPECIFIC INFORMATION

Answers to step 2 (Student's Book page 54)

	Agustín	**Nadezhda**	**Chao**
Country of origin	Mexico	Russia	China
Length of time in the U.S.	over 20 years	4 years	10 years
Reason(s) for coming	to find work	her children: better education	– join his family – study to become a physician's assistant
Difficulties in the beginning	didn't know anyone except for his brother	– hard to leave her country – hard to leave her mother	– hard to work and study at same time – hard to learn English
Life now	– works in a food store – in contact with his family back home	just became a citizen	– loves living in U.S. – studying to make dream come true

INTERVIEW WITH ALVIN, MINSOO, AND ABDOUL-AZIZ: Adapting to life in the United States

Look at the photographs of Alvin, Minsoo, and Abdoul-Aziz and read the vocabulary in the box on page 55 aloud.

LISTENING FOR SPECIFIC INFORMATION

Answers to step 2 (Student's Book page 55–56)

Alvin's family is from Puerto Rico, but he grew up in the States. He describes himself as a hybrid, which is a combination of two cultures. He says he is American on the outside and Puerto Rican inside. At home, he always speaks Spanish, listens to Latin music, and eats Puerto Rican food. When he goes outside, he says he feels as if he is stepping into a different world, so he is constantly going back and forth between two cultures.

Minsoo is from Korea, and she came to the United States five years ago. At home, she speaks Korean. She only speaks English at work and in college. It is difficult for her at college, because she is not used to giving her opinion in class. Minsoo feels that she is half Korean and half American, but she says she is absorbing American culture fast.

Abdoul-Aziz grew up in Niger and came to the United States as an adult. He speaks three languages: English at work and school, French with some of his friends, and Hausa, an African language, with his family. He says it is hard to keep switching languages because it feels like he is constantly changing his identity. He often asks himself: Am I African? Am I American? Or am I a mixture of both?

AFTER THE INTERVIEWS

SHARING YOUR KNOWLEDGE

Review the instructions and encourage students to make connections between their own experience and that of the interviewees.

3 IN YOUR OWN VOICE (Student's Book page 57)

GIVING AN ORAL PRESENTATION

Explain the rationale for giving oral presentations in class: students in the United States, as Minsoo mentioned, are constantly asked to speak in front of their classmates and to present a personal perspective.

Answers to step 1 (Student's Book page 57)

c	**1**
d	**2**
e	**3**
i	**4**
j	**5**
a	**6**
b	**7**
f	**8**
g	**9**
h	**10**

4 ACADEMIC LISTENING AND NOTE TAKING: Recent Immigrants and Today's United States (Student's Book pages 58–64)

BEFORE THE LECTURE

The two topics in this lecture – metaphors describing America's diverse immigrant society and transnationalism, which describes recent immigrants' continuing relationships with their home countries – may need to be defined in simple terms before students begin these tasks. If necessary, elicit metaphors from everyday life from students, beginning with an example of your own. Discuss the meaning of *trans-* as a prefix.

PREVIEWING THE TOPIC

Encourage students to be creative in their responses, and make sure they fully understand the meaning of the four metaphors. Explain that the chart in step 3 shows the varying levels of transnationalism and adaptation of immigrants as they adjust to life in another country.

🎧 NOTE TAKING: LISTENING FOR DEFINITIONS

Answers to step 1 (Student's Book page 59)

1 A metaphor is an image, a picture, or a model that is used to help us understand things that are very complex, like societies.

2 A melting pot is a large metal pot, a kind of container that is used for melting things, such as different foods.

3 A salad is a dish made of different vegetables that are mixed together.

4 A patchwork quilt is a cover for a bed, and it's made from colorful pieces of cloth sewn together.

5 A kaleidoscope is a toy that you look through, and if you turn it, you can see beautiful, changing patterns.

LECTURE, PART ONE: Metaphors for Describing American Society

GUESSING VOCABULARY FROM CONTEXT

Answers to step 2 (Student's Book page 60)

h	**1**
c	**2**
d	**3**
e	**4**
g	**5**
f	**6**
b	**7**
a	**8**

🎧 NOTE TAKING: USING NUMBERS TO ORGANIZE YOUR NOTES

Sample answer to step 2 (Student's Book page 61)

Metaphors for descr. Am. society:

1. Melting pot = pot used for melting foods, etc.
   Ingredients melt together & become someth. new, e.g., fondue
   Acc. to metaphor, imms to U.S. would lose separate ID & mix w/people here.
   Problem w/ metaphor: doesn't describe today's reality, i.e.,
       many imms aren't accepted
       many imms keep parts of their own ID – lang., traditions, marry from
           same ethnic grp, never say they are American.

2. Salad bowl
   Salad = dish made of diff. veg. mixed tog.
   Metaphor represents America as diverse – diff. grps live tog but each grp
       keeps own cult.

3. Patchwork quilt = cover for bed
   Made of colorful cloth sewn tog.
   People like metaphor because we're unique but connected

4. Kaleidoscope = toy w/ changing patterns
   Am = multiracial, multiethnic, multicultural, always changing

---

LECTURE, PART TWO: *Transnationalism*

GUESSING VOCABULARY FROM CONTEXT

Answers to step 2 (Student's Book page 62)

f	1
c	2
b	3
d	4
e	5
a	6

NOTE TAKING: USING BULLETS TO ORGANIZE YOUR NOTES

Sample answers to step 2 (Student's Book page 63)

> Transnationalism = exp going across nations or cultures
>
> 1. Examples
>   • Imms may own homes, land, businesses in country of origin
>   • Send $ to family
>   • Support sports teams back home
>   • Travel home often
>   • Get involved in bus/pol in country of origin
>
> 2. Why?
>   • Ease of travel
>   → People can travel home more often
>   • Technology
>   Stay in contact by phone
>   Easy to send $

AFTER THE LECTURE

SHARING YOUR OPINION

A follow-up activity to this one is to have students write postcards or prepare and give brief presentations describing their own travel experiences. Alternatively, students could write postcards or give presentations describing their own neighborhoods, towns, or cities.

Chapter 4 Lecture Quiz

See the Lecture Quiz section at the back of this Teacher's Manual for a photocopiable quiz on the lecture for Chapter 4. Quiz answers can be found on page 129.

Additional Ideas for Unit 2

Key topics in this unit include diverse cultural and ethnic groups in the United States, the two main waves of immigration in the past two centuries, prejudice against immigrants and contributions they made to American culture, identity, and immigrants' continuing connections to their countries of origin.

1 Have students read stories or a novel about an immigrant group in the United States.

2 Have students research the photographs of Lewis W. Hine (see page 34 of the Student's Book). Alternatively, have students research nineteenth- and early-twentieth-century photographs of people and places in the United States.

3 Ask students to research the #7 subway line in Queens, New York. It was recently named a National Millennium Trail by the U.S. Department of Transportation because it passes through some of the most diverse neighborhoods in the United States.

4 Have students make a list of immigrants in their own neighborhoods or societies, along with a list of the contributions they have made to cultural life.

5 Have students watch a movie about the immigrant experience in the United States, such as *The Namesake*, *The Joy Luck Club*, *My Big Fat Greek Wedding*, or *Quinceañera*.

6 Over the course of a week, have students list the ethnic clothing that they notice people wearing or the ethnic restaurants in their neighborhood or city.

7 Ask students to identify the ways in which *transnationalism* relates to them. For example, do they know a person abroad with whom they have a close relationship? In what ways do they stay in touch?

Unit 3

The Struggle for Equality

Unit Title Page (Student's Book page 65)

Read the title of the unit aloud and discuss the meaning of the words *struggle* and *equality*. Examine the picture that introduces this unit and discuss its relationship to the unit title.

Read the paragraph with students. Discuss the example of inequality in the early days of U.S. history and elicit students' reactions. Make sure that students understand the division between Chapter 5, which focuses mainly on African Americans and women, and Chapter 6, which discusses other groups. Terms and expressions that might require explanation are *discrimination*, *gender*, *civil rights*, and *advanced America's struggle*.

Finally, elicit students' background knowledge on the civil rights movement, the women's movement, and laws promoting equality in the United States.

Chapter 5

The Struggle Begins

Look at the photograph and discuss its relationship to the chapter title and the chapter description on the unit title page.

1 GETTING STARTED (Student's Book pages 66–69)

READING AND THINKING ABOUT THE TOPIC

The introductory passage provides background information that will allow students to contextualize the struggles they will learn about in the chapter. Allow plenty of time to discuss the time frames presented, the "Jim Crow" laws, the significance of World War II for women, the Equal Pay Act, and the Civil Rights Act.

Answers to step 2 (Student's Book page 67)

1 The Civil War; the passage of the Thirteenth, Fourteenth, and Fifteenth Amendments; and the 1954 Supreme Court decision all led to greater equality for African Americans.

2 After the passage of the Nineteenth Amendment, women could vote. Many women worked outside their homes for the first time during World War II.

3 The Civil Rights Act and Equal Pay Act helped both blacks and women. These acts made it illegal to discriminate against workers because of their race or gender, and legalized equal pay for men and women.

🎧 BUILDING BACKGROUND KNOWLEDGE

Look at the photographs on pages 67–69 with students and help them understand the captions, if necessary.

Answers to steps 1 and 2 (Student's Book pages 67–69)

photo	order	date
a	5	1920
b	1	1776
c	6	1954
d	4	1880–1960s
e	2	1848
f	3	1865

2 AMERICAN VOICES: Cynthia and Hilda (Student's Book pages 70–73)

Read the introductory paragraph with students and predict what Cynthia and Hilda might say about their lives.

BEFORE THE INTERVIEWS

BUILDING BACKGROUND KNOWLEDGE

Have students share their responses to the questions before they check the answers at the bottom of page 73. After they have corrected their responses, discuss their reactions.

INTERVIEW WITH CYNTHIA: Before the civil rights movement

Look at the picture of Cynthia and read the items in the box on page 71 aloud.

🎧 LISTENING FOR ANSWERS TO *WH-* QUESTIONS

Sample answers to step 2 (Student's Book page 71)

1 Cynthia was with her parents and brothers and sisters.

2 At a gas station, Cynthia went to drink from a water fountain. The owner grabbed her because the fountain was for whites only.

3 It happened before the civil rights movement.

4 They were going from New York to South Carolina to spend time with family.

5 Cynthia's father couldn't guarantee the family's safety and couldn't protect her.

INTERVIEW WITH HILDA: Before and after the women's movement

Look at the picture of Hilda and read the items in the box on page 72 aloud.

🎧 LISTENING FOR SPECIFIC INFORMATION

Answers to step 2 (Student's Book page 72)

1 b
2 b
3 c
4 a
5 b
6 b

DRAWING INFERENCES

Explain that speakers do not always state their opinions directly, so drawing inferences is an important listening skill. In an academic context, students must also listen to markers, such as tone of voice, in order to reach a conclusion about the intention of the speaker. Give students adequate time to discuss Cynthia and Hilda's stories and relate them to their own lives and experiences.

3 IN YOUR OWN VOICE (Student's Book page 74)

The purpose of these activities is to give students an overview of the presentation process. Explain that doing research, presenting it to classmates, and getting their feedback are common academic tasks.

CONDUCTING RESEARCH

Emphasize the importance of using reputable sources for research, even for extracting basic information. Help students to find and document this information, if necessary, and then encourage them to explore sites or texts about their chosen person more fully.

GIVING AN ORAL PRESENTATION

Remind students that they learned basic strategies for giving oral presentations in Chapter 4. Encourage them to make a visual display of their findings.

RESPONDING TO PRESENTATIONS

Explain that in the United States, students are commonly asked to respond to their classmates' presentations. They should make sure that they ask their questions in a formal and respectful way and listen to others' questions and comments.

4 ACADEMIC LISTENING AND NOTE TAKING: The Civil Rights Movement and the Women's Movement (Student's Book pages 75–80)

BEFORE THE LECTURE

BUILDING BACKGROUND KNOWLEDGE

Have students share their descriptions of the photographs on page 75.

🎧 NOTE TAKING: LISTENING FOR GUIDING QUESTIONS

Answers to steps 1 and 2 (Student's Book page 76)

b	1
a	2
d	3
c	4

LECTURE, PART ONE: *The Civil Rights Movement*

GUESSING VOCABULARY FROM CONTEXT

Answers to step 2 (Student's Book pages 76–77)

d	1
g	2
a	3
c	4
b	5
f	6
e	7

🎧 NOTE TAKING: CREATING YOUR OWN SYMBOLS AND ABBREVIATIONS

It is important to stress that students' answers will vary because they are using symbols and abbreviations that are helpful to them personally. Students might want to compare the symbols and abbreviations that they have chosen.

Sample answers to step 3 (Student's Book page 78)

Pt. 1: The civil rts movt	
What was it?	Strug. by 100s of 1000s of people to achieve eq rts for Af Ams
How did it start?	100 yrs after end of slav., seg + discr still common → beg. of civ rts movt
Key events:	1. Dec 1, 1955: Rosa Parks refused to give up bus seat → Montgomery bus boycott 2. 1960: blk sts refused to leave a rest – owner wouldn't serve b/c of color = sit-ins 3. March 1963: March on Washington 200,000 people heard MLK give "I Have a Dream" speech
What happened next?	More protests, demons, sit-ins – strug to stop prej + discr
Achievements?	1. Jim Crow laws overturned 2. Fed gov't passed laws like Civ Rts Act + Voting Rts Act 3. → other gps began fighting for just + equal

LECTURE, PART TWO: *The Women's Movement*

GUESSING VOCABULARY FROM CONTEXT

Answers to step 2 (Student's Book page 78–79)

b	1
f	2
c	3
e	4
a	5
d	6

NOTE TAKING: ORGANIZING YOUR NOTES IN A CHART

Help students to predict the kind of information they need to listen for as they fill in their chart. Make sure that they understand the symbols and abbreviations that are included in the book, such as ♀, *dissat*, *w/*, *=*, *→*, and *ineq*.

Sample answers to step 2 (Student's Book page 79)

Pt. 2: The women's movt			
WW2	1950s	1960s	Today
♂: fighting in Europe, Asia ♀: took ♂ jobs factories, construction, offices 1945: ♂ came back home → ♀ left jobs	> ♀ started to feel dissat. w/ roles – 30% worked – earned less than ½ of what ♂ earned for = job – could be teachers, nurses, secs – no ♀ managers	1963: journalist Betty Friedan wrote bk Book showed ♀ unhappy w/ lives → beg. of women's movt Mid 1960s: women demanded = opps	Successes of WM: – = pay for = wk – more ♀ than ♂ in college – more control over lives But: – today ♀ make only 87¢ for $1 ♂ make – 12 weeks out of work for baby Ineq. still exists

AFTER THE LECTURE

REVIEWING YOUR NOTES AFTER A LECTURE

Stress to students the importance of reviewing notes soon after a lecture. This is to make sure they can read and understand the symbols and abbreviations they created, identify questions they have about the content, and fill in missing information. Encourage students from both groups to share the information they have learned.

Chapter 5 Lecture Quiz

See the Lecture Quiz section at the back of this Teacher's Manual for a photocopiable quiz on the lecture for Chapter 5. Quiz answers can be found on page 130.

Chapter 6

The Struggle Continues

Look at the photograph and discuss its relationship to the chapter title and the chapter description on the unit title page.

1 **GETTING STARTED** (Student's Book pages 81–82)

READING AND THINKING ABOUT THE TOPIC

This paragraph is about progress toward greater equality in the United States and the need to make further improvements in this area. It explains how the successes of the 1960s led other groups to struggle for greater equality. Students might want to discuss the reasons why ethnic studies programs, access to public services, and school assistance for children with disabilities are such important milestones in this struggle. Finally, make sure that students have the chance to discuss the present state of prejudice against people of different ethnicities, sexes, ages, and abilities, and to share their opinions about stereotypes and tolerance.

Answers to step 2 (Student's Book page 82)

1 Groups that have struggled for equality since the 1960s include Hispanics, older people, and people with disabilities.

2 The protests of Latinos have led to ethnic studies programs at U.S. colleges. Older Americans are guaranteed more access to public services. Public schools must provide assistance to children with disabilities.

3 Racism, sexism, ageism, and prejudice against people with disabilities still exist. Laws have been passed, but they are not always enforced or renewed.

🎧 LISTENING FOR SPECIFIC INFORMATION

Answers to step 2 (Student's Book page 82)

1 Peter is 55 years old. Five months ago, he lost his job as a computer programmer because the company didn't have enough work for him. But then the company hired a new programmer who is 26 years old.

2 Theresa is a journalist. Last week she had an interview for a job with a magazine. It went well until the end, when the interviewer asked her if she was pregnant. She said yes. She didn't get the job.

3 Robert is married and has three children. Last week, he and his wife filled out an application for a new apartment. However, they didn't get it. A friend told them it's because nobody else in the building has children, and the manager is worried about noise.

4 Rebecca is a university student who uses a wheelchair. One of her classes is on the 8th floor and the building has only two elevators, so she has been late to class a few times. She explained the problem to her professor, but he expects her to come to class on time just like everyone else.

2 AMERICAN VOICES: Robin, Jairo, and Sandy

(Student's Book pages 83–87)

BEFORE THE INTERVIEWS

The most important part of this activity is the students' reaction to the information (answers are at the bottom of page 83 of the Student's Book). Allow time for students to explain their guesses and their opinions about the information.

BUILDING BACKGROUND KNOWLEDGE

Look at the picture of Robin and read the vocabulary items in the box on page 84 aloud.

INTERVIEW WITH ROBIN: Working with the blind

🎧 LISTENING FOR SPECIFIC INFORMATION

Sample answers to steps 2 and 3 (Student's Book page 84–85)

a Computers that talk allow blind people to have access to information that they wouldn't be able to see.

b Braille printouts of documents allow blind people to exchange information.

c A talking clock is a simple device that says the time aloud.

d Trays help keep things together. If someone puts something down, he or she can find it again quickly.

e A bill that is folded a certain way allows blind people to tell how much it is worth.

INTERVIEW WITH JAIRO AND SANDY: The struggle of two groups for equality

Look at the pictures of Jairo and Sandy and read the vocabulary items on page 85 aloud.

🎧 LISTENING FOR MAIN IDEAS

Sample answers to step 2 (Student's Book page 85)

	Group	Progress toward equality	Problems that still exist
Jairo	Latinos	– Latinos recog at every level → sports, entertainment, educ – Latinos in gov: mayors, Cong – many services now avail in Span + other langs	– poverty in the Hisp comm – access to health care or high quality educ
Sandy	senior citizens	– illeg to discr against people because of age – hiring and firing	– laws hard to enforce

AFTER THE INTERVIEWS

SHARING YOUR OPINION

Sample answers to step 2 (Student's Book page 86)

1 Most people make boundaries and classify others. This limits the groups you can spend time with.

2 According to Pebbles, people are very concerned about appearance. Because of this, they don't see the good or bad in people.

3 When people are not accepted, they feel sad. They stay with the only group of people who do accept them.

4 Social boundaries are like bags that we tie different groups up in. Pebbles thinks that these "little bags" limit your friendships.

5 Pebbles thinks that people should mix with different groups of people to have more friends.

3 IN YOUR OWN VOICE (Student's Book pages 88–89)

THINKING CRITICALLY ABOUT THE TOPIC

Although the goal of this activity is to make a presentation about what the groups have learned about tolerance, allow plenty of time for the three steps and encourage students to collaborate with others in their group. Remind students that critical thinking involves exchanging ideas and considering different viewpoints. Students should be able to choose the activity that most interests them, whether it is examining gender roles in magazines, analyzing a quotation about tolerance, or sharing a personal experience of discrimination.

GIVING AN ORAL PRESENTATION

Students have engaged in this activity before, but this time they are being asked to share – as a group – the results of a prolonged group activity. Stress the importance of teamwork and of giving everyone in the group a chance to participate in the activity.

4 ACADEMIC LISTENING AND NOTE TAKING: Two Important Laws in the Struggle for Equality (Student's Book pages 90–96)

BEFORE THE LECTURE

SHARING YOUR OPINION

Look at the photographs with the students. Elicit and discuss some challenges and difficulties that senior citizens and disabled people often face.

NOTE TAKING: LISTENING FOR SIGNAL WORDS AND PHRASES

Answers to step 2 (Student's Book page 91–92)
1 To refresh your memory
2 first / third
3 Before
4 In other words
5 In addition
6 also / because
7 as for
8 the most important
9 because

LECTURE, PART ONE: The Age Discrimination in Employment Act

GUESSING VOCABULARY FROM CONTEXT

Answers to step 2 (Student's Book page 92)

b	1
d	2
c	3
f	4
e	5
a	6
g	7
h	8

🎧 NOTE TAKING: INDENTING

Sample answer to step 3 (Student's Book page 93)

Age Discrim. in Employment Act

1. Why law was needed
    - Older people faced discrim. in wkplace:
       Before law, employers could set age limits, e.g., 35

2. What the law does
    - Protects people > 40 from discrim.
    - Can't use age to:
       • refuse to hire
       • fire
       • promote to a better position

3. Impact of law
    - nowadays, nothing about age in job app
    - equal benefits for older + younger people
    - no mandatory retirement

4. Do employers follow law?
    - 1000s of complaints per year → age discrim. still exists
    - Recent study showed companies 40% more likely to interview
       younger applicant
    - But: People are more aware of age discrim. than before law

---

LECTURE, PART TWO: The Americans with Disabilities Act

GUESSING VOCABULARY FROM CONTEXT

Answers to step 2 (Student's Book page 94)

d	1
c	2
b	3
e	4
g	5
a	6
f	7

⌒ NOTE TAKING: USING AN OUTLINE

Sample answer to step 4 (Student's Book page 95)

The Americans with Disabilities Act (ADA)

I.   ADA
    A. Passed in 1990
    B. Protects ppl w/ disabil. in diff places, e.g.,
        1. work
        2. housing
        3. educ.

II. Def. of "disability"
    A. Physical
    B. Mental

III. Impact of ADA
    A. Changed life for disabled people, e.g.,
        1. buses have mechanisms to help ppl in wheelchairs
        2. doorways must be wide
        3. some businesses hiring ppl w/ nonphysical (mental) disab
        4. sts w/ learning disab can get more time on tests

    B. Most important impact of law: Change ppl's thinking
        1. Some countries: Disabled stay home b/c no way to get around
        2. U.S.: Understand there are many things disabled ppl can do
          – Pres. Bush (1990) said: "Let the shameful wall of exclusion finally come tumbling down."
        3. Goal must be inclusion

AFTER THE LECTURE

USING YOUR NOTES TO MAKE A TIME LINE

Explain to students that the visual representation of a time line is helpful for organizing and remembering historical information and dates.

Chapter 6 Lecture Quiz

See the Lecture Quiz section at the back of this Teacher's Manual for a photocopiable quiz on the lecture for Chapter 6. Quiz answers can be found on page 130.

Additional Ideas for Unit 3

This unit is about the struggle for equality of different groups in the United States, including African Americans, women, the elderly, and the disabled. It also discusses significant social and political movements, such as the civil rights movement and the women's movement, and laws that guarantee equal rights.

1 Have students use the Internet or a library to research photographs of some of the important events discussed in this unit, including the Emancipation Proclamation, the Civil War, *Brown vs Board of Education* protests, the Montgomery bus boycott, sit-ins, the March on Washington, and so on. Ask students to share their knowledge about the events shown in the photographs and their reactions to what they see.

2 Have students identify important political and social movements today and/or struggles by groups that currently feel they are disadvantaged.

3 Ask students to research the impact of Live Aid, a multi-venue rock concert to promote equality, attended or watched by 1.5 billion people in 100 countries. Alternatively, have them research the life of a musician who was active during the 1960s, such as John Lennon, Joan Baez, or Bob Dylan, who used music as a form of protest. Have students explain what they find to the class.

4 Have students watch a segment of *Eyes on the Prize*, a documentary about the Civil Rights Movement.

5 Ask students to read an excerpt from *The Feminine Mystique* by Betty Friedan.

6 Have students watch all or a segment of *Iron Jawed Angels*, a film about the women's suffrage movement in the early 1900s.

7 Have students listen to Dr. Martin Luther King, Jr.'s "I Have a Dream" speech online.

8 If they haven't already done so, have students research the women of Gee's Bend. (See page 162 of the Student's Book.)

Unit **4**

American Values

Unit Title Page (Student's Book page 97)

Read the title of the unit. Elicit and discuss with students the values that they consider American. Then discuss the photograph and elicit students' reactions. Read the unit summary paragraph with students. Make sure they understand the progression from Chapter 7, which discusses traditional values that form the foundation of American culture, to Chapter 8, which considers ways these values may have changed in modern America.

   Make sure students understand the concept of *folk heroes*, the topic of the lecture in Chapter 7. Point out by way of example some folk heroes that are important in your students' own community. Then discuss the topic of the lecture in Chapter 8: conservative and liberal political views in America. Answer any questions about the terms *conservative* and *liberal*.

Chapter 7

American Values from the Past

Look at the photograph and discuss its relationship to the chapter title and the chapter description on the unit title page.

1 GETTING STARTED (Student's Book pages 98–99)

READING AND THINKING ABOUT THE TOPIC

The introductory paragraph discusses the importance and origin of American values. Terms that might require attention include *Greek and Roman civilizations*, *Judaism*, and *Christianity*. Students might also have questions about the "Protestant work ethic." It is worth spending time discussing the significance of the values that are mentioned in the paragraph: hard work, self-reliance, equality, freedom, individualism, and democracy.

Answers to step 2 (Student's Book page 99)
1 Values are beliefs that help us decide what is right and wrong and how we should behave in various situations. They guide our personal, social, and business behavior and affect every aspect of our daily lives.
2 Greek and Roman civilizations and the religious beliefs of Judaism and Christianity, particularly the Protestant tradition, have influenced American values.
3 Some key American values are: hard work, self-reliance, equality, freedom, individualism, and democracy.

⌒ LISTENING FOR SPECIFIC INFORMATION

Answers to step 2 (Student's Book page 99)
1 Ben
2 have died
3 has few friends, but he refuses to lose hope
4 positive
5 rich stranger
6 Harvard University
7 good luck and determination

2 AMERICAN VOICES: Marielena, Dan, Anne-Marie, and Leila (Student's Book pages 100–104)

BEFORE THE INTERVIEWS

BUILDING VOCABULARY

Answers to step 1 (Student's Book page 100)

c	1
a	2
d	3
f	4
b	5
g	6
e	7
k	8
l	9
j	10
h	11
m	12
i	13

INTERVIEW WITH MARIELENA AND DAN: Personal values

Look at the pictures of Marielena and Dan and read aloud the vocabulary items in the box on page 101.

⌒ ANSWERING TRUE/FALSE/NOT SURE QUESTIONS

1, 2 | Review the instructions with your students and explain that sometimes, there is not enough information given to answer a question with certainty.

Answers to step 2 (Student's Book page 102)
Marielena

F	1	Marielena says the most important value is independence.
NI	2	We know that she has a daughter, but she may or may not have a son.
F	3	Her daughter is 12.
NI	4	We do not know if there are many artists in her family.
T	5	

Dan

- F **1** The values Dan mentions are hard work and self-reliance.
- NI **2** We do not know how old Dan is.
- T **3**
- NI **4** We do not know if Dan wants to go to graduate school.
- F **5** Dan's part-time job is in a bookstore.

INTERVIEW WITH ANNE-MARIE AND LEILA: Disagreeing with traditional values

Look at the pictures of Anne-Marie and Leila and read the vocabulary items in the box on page 103.

🎧 LISTENING FOR MAIN IDEAS

Answers to step 2 (Student's Book page 103)

1 L **a**
    A-M **b**

2 L **a**
    L **b**
    A-M **c**
    L **d**
    A-M **e**

AFTER THE INTERVIEWS

SHARING YOUR OPINION

This exercise provides several opportunities for students to explain their opinions clearly. They may also want to provide examples from their personal experience. You may want to compare answers as a class. There could be disagreements among class members, giving students the opportunity to engage in a prolonged discussion and explanation of their viewpoints.

3 IN YOUR OWN VOICE (Student's Book page 105)

GIVING AN ORAL PRESENTATION

Students might need assistance either in understanding the vocabulary in this task, such as *trying times*, *punctuality*, *tact*, etc., or in grasping the meaning of the sayings. Once they have fully understood them, prompt students to add experiences from their own life that illustrate their meaning. Some students may also wish to share similar sayings from another language, translated into English.

4 ACADEMIC LISTENING AND NOTE TAKING: Three American Folk Heroes (Student's Book pages 106–111)

BEFORE THE LECTURE

SHARING YOUR KNOWLEDGE

Look at the pictures with your students and give them time to describe and react to what they see. Ask them if they see a connection between the images.

🎧 NOTE TAKING: LISTENING FOR KEY WORDS

Answers to step 1 (Student's Book page 107)
1 folk heroes / folk heroes
2 cowboy / cowboys / cowboy / cowboy
3 entrepreneur / entrepreneurs / entrepreneur
4 superheroes / superheroes

LECTURE, PART ONE: Three American Folk Heroes

GUESSING VOCABULARY FROM CONTEXT

Answers to step 2 (Student's Book page 108)

a	1
g	2
f	3
d	4
c	5
e	6
b	7

NOTE TAKING: CLARIFYING YOUR NOTES

Sample answer to step 2 (Student's Book page 109)

Intro Topic: 3 (folk heroes) = people or ???? do (extrord.) things or have extrord. powers 3 famous ones = cowboy, ???, + superhero Rep. our most imp. values	*imaginary figures* *extraordinary* *entrepreneur*

1. Cowboy
  See everywhere: TV, advert., fashion
 	
  Why so popular?
    150 yrs ago, people moved west to make ?
    Some started catel (sp?) ranches, hired c'boys to help
    C'boy became hero b/c work alone, self-reliant*
 	
    Cowboy rep' values: _courage_, freedom, _independence_
	their fortune
	cattle
	self-reliant =
	independent

2. Entrepreneur
  = starts company → profit
  = gt. ideas, risks
  = symbol of Am. values
  Smart + wk hard + good ideas → succeed
  Pop. since Horatio Alger stories
  Ex. Bill Gates	

3. Superhero
  Many kinds: Superman, Batman, Spiderman, etc.
  Fast, powerful, symbols of justice + law
  Defend good, punish bad	

LECTURE, PART TWO: Questions and answers

GUESSING VOCABULARY FROM CONTEXT

Answers to step 2 (Student's Book page 109)

d	**1**
b	**2**
c	**3**
e	**4**
a	**5**

∩ NOTE TAKING: TAKING NOTES ON QUESTIONS AND ANSWERS

Sample answers to step 2 (Student's Book page 110)

1. Entrepreneur
   After Civil War, indust. exp
   U.S. railroads grew → steel/oil indus grew
   Ex. Carnegie, mills of $$ from steel
   Ex. Rockefeller → oil

2. Superman
   Written 1930s – still pop.
   Other superheroes came later
   Ex. *The Incredibles* – one of most profit. movies → $500 mill

3. Women folk heroes
   Very few
   Annie Oakley in 19c famous for shooting
   Wonder Woman in 1941
   Most trad. folk heroes = men

AFTER THE LECTURE

SHARING YOUR OPINION

1,2 Allow students plenty of time to read the stories, discuss them, and list the values that they think the people in the stories have.

3 Prompt students to provide an elaborate description of a person whom they consider a personal hero or who has inspired them in some way. Make sure they give examples of the values that the person has. You may want to ask a few students to share their story with the class.

Chapter 7 Lecture Quiz

See the Lecture Quiz section at the back of this Teacher's Manual for a photocopiable quiz on the lecture for Chapter 7. Quiz answers can be found on page 131.

Chapter 8

American Values Today

Look at the photograph and discuss its relationship to the chapter title and the chapter description on the unit title page. Ask students to compare this photograph with the one at the beginning of Chapter 7, on page 98. Elicit from students how the photographs are related.

 GETTING STARTED (Student's Book pages 112–114)

READING AND THINKING ABOUT THE TOPIC

Read the introductory passage with students and make sure they understand the concept of the generations mentioned in the chapter (Baby Boomers, Generation X, Generation Y) and the descriptions of political philosophies. Also, make sure they understand how disagreements can arise because of people's different political viewpoints.

Answers to step 2 (Student's Book page 113)
1 The three generations described are the Baby Boomers, people born between the end of World War II and the mid-1960s; Generation X, people born between the mid-1960s and mid-1970s; and Generation Y, people born during the late 1970s and the 1980s.
2 These three generations tend to have different values because of the world events and technological innovations that happened during their lives.
3 Conservatives tend to believe in keeping traditional cultural and religious values and oppose sudden change. Liberals tend to favor reform and progress more than tradition.

SHARING YOUR KNOWLEDGE

Answers to step 1 (Student's Book page 113)

1   Y   a
    X   b
  BB   c

2   BB   a
    Y   b
    X   c

3   Y   a
  BB   b
    X   c

🎧 LISTENING FOR SPECIFIC INFORMATION

Answers to step 2 (Student's Book page 114)

Information to listen for	Notes
Size of Generation Y	Between 70 and 76 million
Percentage of U.S. population	About 20 percent of the U.S. population
Six times as big as:	Generation X
Values of Generation Y	Tolerance for diversity; speed and constant change; independence; money; social responsibility

2   AMERICAN VOICES: Rosiane, Dan-el, Christine, and Sandy

(Student's Book pages 115–119)

Read the introductory paragraph with the class and look at the photographs on page 116. Ask students to guess the generations of the interviewees.

BEFORE THE INTERVIEWS

SHARING YOUR OPINION

Ask a few students to share the information from the Venn diagram with the class.

INTERVIEW WITH ROSIANE, DAN-EL, AND CHRISTINE: Differences in values between parents and children

Look at the pictures of Rosiane, Dan-el, and Christine on page 116 and read aloud the vocabulary in the box on page 115.

🎧 DRAWING INFERENCES

Answers to step 1 (Student's Book page 116)

1   R   a   2   R   a
   C   b   D   b
   D   c   C   c
   C   d
   R   e
   R   f

Answers to step 2 (Student's Book pages 116–117)
1 Christine
2 Dan-el's mother/father
3 Rosiane
4 Dan-el
5 Rosiane's mother/father
6 Christine's mother/father

INTERVIEW WITH SANDY: Values in the workplace

Look at the picture of Sandy on page 118 and read aloud the vocabulary in the box on page 117.

🎧 LISTENING FOR SPECIFIC INFORMATION

Sample answers to step 1 (Student's Book page 118)
1 She is a business professor.
2 She asks her students: "If you had your own business, would you hire you?"
3 She says that not respecting deadlines is unacceptable because "time is money."
4 She asks students to imagine that they are buying a car. They have paid the deposit, but then they are told that they won't get their car for another week.
5 The second value she teaches is cooperation and working as a team. This is important because in the workplace, people don't work in isolation.
6 She says students should have a professional attitude, and they should dress, speak, and write in an appropriate way. They should use a formal tone when speaking and writing.

ROLE PLAYING

1 | **Sample answers** (Student's Book page 118)
  a Sandy would probably say no. She has already explained that people in the workplace don't work in isolation.
  b She would probably say no. She stresses that it is important to respect deadlines.
  c She would probably say that it isn't OK to skip class and ask the student to use a more professional and appropriate tone.

2 | Encourage students to exercise their creativity in the role play.

AFTER THE INTERVIEWS

SHARING YOUR OPINION

Allow students to explain their viewpoints fully and encourage them to explain any disagreements they might have. Ask students to give examples to support their opinion.

3 IN YOUR OWN VOICE (Student's Book pages 120–121)

CONDUCTING A SURVEY

Read the introductory passage aloud and review the importance of doing an out-of-class survey. Make sure students understand the steps involved: identifying possible interviewees of different ages, noting whether they are male or female, and then asking follow-up questions to get details about the interviewees' opinions.

When the surveys have been completed, allow enough time to review the questions in step 3: the differences between the responses of older and younger people, the three items that the interviewees value most, and the most interesting answer the interviewees gave to the students' follow-up questions.

4 ACADEMIC LISTENING AND NOTE TAKING: Conservative and Liberal Values in American Politics (Student's Book pages 122–128)

BEFORE THE LECTURE

Remind students of their discussion at the beginning of the unit about the meaning of the terms *conservative* and *liberal*.

BUILDING BACKGROUND KNOWLEDGE

Facilitate this paired information-sharing task and assist with the pronunciation of the presidents' names.

🎧 NOTE TAKING: LISTENING FOR GENERAL STATEMENTS

Answers to step 2 (Student's Book page 123)
1 But even though people's values are very diverse, the strongest voices in American politics today do **generally** fall into two groups – conservative and liberal.
2 Conservatives **usually** put a strong emphasis on personal responsibility.
3 **Most** liberals, on the other hand, think the government should be very active in fixing social problems like poverty and illness.
4 **Generally**, conservatives think government is too big and expensive.
5 Conservatives **typically** believe that the government should stay out of the way of business.
6 **But in general**, liberals believe that government should control and regulate business through strict laws or taxes.
7 The U.S. has two main political parties, so in an election, voters **generally** choose between the Republicans and the Democrats.

LECTURE, PART ONE: *Conservative and liberal values*

GUESSING VOCABULARY FROM CONTEXT

Answers to step 2 (Student's Book page 124)

e	**1**
a	**2**
f	**3**
b	**4**
d	**5**
g	**6**
c	**7**

🎧 NOTE TAKING: TAKING NOTES IN A POINT-BY-POINT FORMAT

Sample answer to step 2 (Student's Book page 125)

Conserv./Lib. Values	
1. Role of gov't	Conserv: Not gov't resp. to pay for social progs. Lib: Gov't should fix soc. prob's like poverty + illness
2. Taxes	Conserv: Gov't is too big + expen. High taxes unpop. Lib: Taxes nec. to support soc. progs.
3. Business	Conserv: Gov't shouldn't interfere w/ biz: econ. w/o gov't control can grow Lib: Gov't should control + reg. biz Ex: If not reg'd, entreprs won't care about wkrs or custs or envir, only profit

LECTURE, PART TWO: *Values and Political Parties*

GUESSING VOCABULARY FROM CONTEXT

Answers to step 2 (Student's Book page 126)

b	**1**
g	**2**
a	**3**
c	**4**
i	**5**
h	**6**
e	**7**
f	**8**
d	**9**

🎧 NOTE TAKING: USING A HANDOUT TO HELP YOU TAKE NOTES

Sample answer to step 2 (Student's Book page 127)

Values + Pol. Parties

I.   Intro
    A. U.S. has 2-party system
    B. In gen: Repub = conserve.
                Dem = lib.
    C. But: ideas change over time

II. Election results
    A. 1964: 90% voted for Dem, Johnson
    B. 1984: Dramatic → 97% voted for Repub, Reagan
    C. 2000: ½ and ½

III. Why do changes happen?
    A. Econ. conditions
        ex. good econ. w/ Reagan → 2nd term
    B. Concern about international sit.
        ex. G.W. Bush
    C. New gens of voters have diff. values

IV. Conc: Can only discuss in gen way – all 50 states "purple"

AFTER THE LECTURE

SHARING YOUR OPINION

1, 2 | Emphasize to students the lecturer's main point: We can talk about these things only in a general way. Therefore, responses to the questions indicate a *general* liberal or conservative viewpoint. Point out that many people hold liberal opinions on some questions and conservative opinions on others.

3 | Give students plenty of time to share their opinions with each other.

Chapter 8 Lecture Quiz

See the Lecture Quiz section at the back of this Teacher's Manual for a photocopiable quiz on the lecture for Chapter 8. Quiz answers can be found on page 131.

Additional Ideas for Unit 4

This unit traces the development of the values that have defined the United States throughout its history. Traditional values discussed include the work ethic, self-reliance, and individualism. The unit also deals with the topic of conservative and liberal values in America as well as American folk heroes and the ways in which they exemplify the values Americans believe in.

1 Have students identify the folk heroes that have most influenced the culture they are most familiar with.

2 Identify values that are either very similar to or different from the American values discussed in this unit.

3 Ask students to listen online to a speech by an American President or read the speech in a book. Ask them to identify the values that the President refers to.

4 Have students watch a contemporary movie made in the United States and list all the main values discussed in this unit that are reflected in the movie. Then ask them to share their observations with other students.

5 Ask students to discuss the ways in which the following groups may have different values: a) older and younger people; b) urban and rural dwellers; c) manual workers and professionals; d) men and women; e) immigrants and nonimmigrants.

Spotlight on Culture

Unit Title Page (Student's Book page 129)

Read the title of the unit aloud and discuss the key words *spotlight* and *culture*. Then look at the collage and discuss its relationship to the unit title.

Chapter 9 focuses on American innovations. Although the term *innovation* is elaborated in the chapter itself, spend a few minutes defining this word and discussing students' ideas about it. Then draw their attention to the topics of the chapter: digital technology, sports, and movies, as well as the musical genres that form the content of the lecture.

Chapter 10 involves the transformation of products and practices that have become popular in countries other than the ones in which they originated. In today's interconnected world, it is often hard to determine the origin of such products and practices, yet students may be able to think of examples from their own experience.

Chapter 9

American Innovations

Look at the collage and discuss its relationship to the chapter title and the chapter description on the unit title page.

1 GETTING STARTED (Student's Book pages 130–131)

READING AND THINKING ABOUT THE TOPIC

This passage explains the difference between an invention and an innovation and articulates some of the reasons why Americans value innovation so highly. It goes on to explain some areas of life that innovation affects.

Answers to step 2 (Student's Book page 131)

1 Innovation is the act or process of producing something new. It includes using an existing product (invention) in a new or different way and making it available to a larger number of people.

2 Americans value innovation in daily life: in the way they live, work, and study, as well as in their cultural life.

LISTENING FOR SPECIFIC INFORMATION

Answers to step 2 (Student's Book p. 131)
1. 1800, Italy
2. 1974, United States
3. 1888, United States
4. 1974, United States
5. 1940s, United States
6. 1975, United States
7. 1920, United States
8. 1961, South Africa
9. 1933, Great Britain
10. 1930s, United States

2 AMERICAN VOICES: Cristina, Victor, Ronnie, and Mara
(Student's Book pages 132–136)

BEFORE THE INTERVIEWS

SHARING YOUR OPINION

> Use the items on the list to generate discussion about the process of innovation and discuss the items that they replaced, if any. For example, cell phones replaced land lines. They are now practically ubiquitous; in fact, some people no longer have a land line. They are preferred because of their convenience and cost, as well as flexibility of options and access to rapidly evolving digital technology. Now, for example, some cell phones can be used to access the Internet, purchase tickets, take digital photos, and download music.

BUILDING BACKGROUND KNOWLEDGE

Answers (Student's Book page 132)

c	1
d	2
g	3
b	4
a	5
e	6
f	7

INTERVIEW WITH CRISTINA AND VICTOR: Using digital technology

Look at the pictures of Cristina and Victor and read aloud the vocabulary items in the box on page 133.

🎧 ANSWERING MULTIPLE CHOICE QUESTIONS

Answers to step 2 (Student's Book pages 133–134)

1 c
2 b
3 b
4 b
5 c
6 c
7 b
8 b
9 a
10 b

INTERVIEW WITH RONNIE AND MARA: Innovations in sports and movies

Look at the pictures of Ronnie and Mara on page 135 and read aloud the vocabulary in the box on page 134.

🎧 DRAWING INFERENCES

Explain that because making inferences involves going beyond what is directly stated, it is possible for students to have different answers, depending on how they interpret a person's words. The answers below are suggestions. Encourage students to explain their answers and disagree with each other, if they wish.

Sample answers to step 3 (Student's Book page 135)

Ronnie

L	1	We do not know this for a fact, but Ronnie mentions many sports: soccer, rugby, baseball, basketball, and so on. He also implies that he participates in sporting activities on a regular basis. It is therefore likely to assume that he is good at sports, although he does not say this directly.
L	2	Ronnie does not say that he prefers team sports to individual sports, but the first four sports he mentions (soccer, rugby, baseball, basketball) are all team sports.
U	3	Although Ronnie does say that he saw the winter Olympics on TV, it is unlikely that he spends a lot of time watching TV, since he spends so much time outdoors playing sports.
L	4	Ronnie mentions the fact that most extreme sports are dangerous and many people get hurt doing them.
?	5	Ronnie is not sure whether he will try snowboarding one day because of the danger and the need for specialized equipment. However, he does express interest in doing so.

Mara

  L   **6** Mara expresses familiarity with many genres and says she likes film a lot. Unless she owns the movies, it is likely that she rents them.

  L   **7** Mara's interest in special effects and computer animation suggests that she knows something about how movies are made, although she does not say this directly.

  ?   **8** Mara does not mention recommending movies to her friends, although it is possible that she does so.

  ?   **9** Mara mentions both serious and playful movies, but it is not possible to say whether she prefers one over the other.

  U   **10** Mara likes all kinds of films, and says that old black and white films sometimes have better stories than modern ones.

AFTER THE INTERVIEWS

DISCUSSING PROS AND CONS

Answers to step 1 (Student's Book page 136)

Speaker	Innovation	Pros	Cons
Cristina	Computer	Search engines help her find information quickly. She uses her computer for many purposes.	Early computers were hard to use. Her e-mail is full of spam. People always bother her.
	iPod	You can download music from the Internet	X
	Cell phone	X	Cell phones are annoying and intrusive. They allow you no privacy.
Victor	Computer (laptop)	He uses his computer for everything. It is especially useful for college. It saves time.	Sometimes he can't think clearly in front of a screen. Sitting in front of a computer can be uncomfortable. It is easy to waste time on the computer.
Ronnie	Extreme sports	They are fast, fun, and trendy.	You need special equipment. They can be dangerous.
Mara	Special effects	They are advanced and innovative. They can be very realistic.	Modern movies rely so much on special effects that sometimes the plot and the acting aren't good.

3 IN YOUR OWN VOICE (Student's Book page 137)

CONDUCTING RESEARCH

Remind students of the need to properly document their sources, even if the research they are doing is quite basic. If necessary, go over a few basic formats for documenting sources.

Answers to step 1

Clothing	Household items	Medicine
jeans cowboy boots	coffee pot sewing machine lightbulb	robotic surgery artificial heart
Music	**Industry**	**Office equipment**
blues jazz	assembly-line production power tools	Scotch® tape

4 ACADEMIC LISTENING AND NOTE TAKING: The Blues and Country Music: Two American Musical Genres

(Student's Book pages 138–143)

Read the introductory statement aloud with students and make sure they understand the word *genres*. Point out that both the blues and country music are American in origin.

BEFORE THE LECTURE

SHARING YOUR KNOWLEDGE

Answers to step 1 (Student's Book page 138)

Genres	Places of origin	Themes	Instruments	Musicians

blues
country
	Appalachia
	Mississippi
	   Delta
		cruelty
		devotion
		loyalty
		lost love
			banjo
			bass
			drums
			guitar
			harmonica
			piano
			saxophone
			violin
				Bessie Smith
				Dixie Chicks
				Robert
				   Johnson
				Willie Nelson

🎧 NOTE TAKING: LISTENING FOR SIMILARITIES AND DIFFERENCES

Answers to step 2 (Student's Book page 139)

1 Like
2 similarity
3 similarities / distinct
4 different / than
5 While / same
6 difference / different
7 Unlike

LECTURE, PART ONE: The blues

GUESSING VOCABULARY FROM CONTEXT

Answers to steps 1 and 2 (Student's Book pages 139–140)

    _a_ **1**
    _c_ **2**
    _d_ **3**
    _b_ **4**
    _e_ **5**

NOTE TAKING: CHOOSING A FORMAT FOR YOUR NOTES

Make sure students understand that note taking is a personal activity and that ultimately, they should choose the format that suits them best at the time they are listening to a particular lecture. Sometimes, a lecturer will make the format of the lecture very clear at the beginning of the lecture itself. More frequently, however, students must work quickly to figure out which of the formats is best suited to what they are hearing. Charts, columns, maps, and outlines are four easy formats that can be adapted to almost every lecture and allow the same information to be recorded in a variety of styles.

Review the formats with students and discuss the differences between them. Elicit students' reactions and preferences. Discuss any advantages and disadvantages students see for each.

Finally, stress that notes, no matter how carefully taken, should be reviewed soon after the lecture so that students can easily identify main ideas and supporting details and examples; extract important names, dates, and other specifics; and clarify points that they did not understand.

Sample answer to step 2 (Student's Book page 140)

> **Two genres of Am.** ♩
>
> I. Blues
>   A. Origin
>   1. name: "having the blues" – feeling sad/troubled/melancholy
>   2. orig w/ freed Af slaves, children, etc. in Miss. "Delta"
>   3. when?? – slave songs, first recs at beg. of 20th c
>   B. Musical elements
>   1. instruments
>   a. single singer w/ guitar/banjo
>   b. other instr later
>   (1) piano
>   (2) harmonica
>   2. themes: lost love, poverty, cruelty
>   C. Famous musicians – Robert Johnson
>   1. most imp. blues mus.
>   2. only 29 songs
>   3. died at 26
>   D. Development
>   1. blues moved to cities, became pop.
>   2. influenced other mus. genres
>   a. jazz
>   b. R&B
>   c. RnR

LECTURE, PART TWO: Country Music

GUESSING VOCABULARY FROM CONTEXT

Answers to steps 1 and 2 (Student's Book page 142)

d	1
b	2
c	3
e	4
a	5

🎧 NOTE TAKING: CHOOSING A FORMAT FOR YOUR NOTES

Have students share the formats they selected for Part One of the lecture. Then have them continue their notes in the same format. Draw their attention to the map at the top of page 142 of the Student's Book. The map will help them picture the parts of the United States the lecturer refers to.

Sample answer (Student's Book page 142)

II. Country
    A. Origin
        1. infl. by early blues, black church mus., Br folk mus.
        2. name: from descs of white Eur imms
        3. orig in rural areas, esp. Tenn, Vir, Ken
    B. Musical elements
        1. themes
            a. some sad, some positive
            b. devot. to home / family
            c. f'dom and indep.
            d. love of land
        2. gps of mus and singers, not just 1
        3. sung in harmony
        4. instruments
            a. guitars – now also elec.
            b. banjos
            c. piano – now also elec.
            d. drums
            e. violin
            f. bass
            g. mandolin
    C. Development – most pop genre in U.S. today
    D. Famous musicians
        1. Willie Nelson (active 1950s +) – nat'l treas
        2. Faith Hill
        3. Dixie Chicks

AFTER THE LECTURE

USING YOUR NOTES TO MAKE NOTE CARDS (Student's Book page 143)

Have students select the information they wish to review. Items could include: Appalachian states, famous blues or country musicians, typical instruments, etc.

Make this last activity an interactive mechanism for reviewing the information students have learned as well as for sharing their opinion about the music they listened to.

Chapter 9 Lecture Quiz

See the Lecture Quiz section at the back of this Teacher's Manual for a photocopiable quiz on the lecture for Chapter 9. Quiz answers can be found on page 132.

Chapter 10

Global Transformations

Look at the photograph and discuss its relationship to the chapter title and the chapter description on the unit title page.

1 GETTING STARTED (Student's Book pages 144–145)

READING AND THINKING ABOUT THE TOPIC

The passage explains the concepts of globalization and global transformation and provides examples of the kinds of transformations of products and ideas this chapter will discuss. Elicit students' thoughts about global transformations they have noticed in their own lives. If your class is heterogeneous, an easy and fun example is the types of menu items found at McDonald's in different parts of the world.

Answers to step 2 (Student's Book page 145)

1 Globalization describes the close economic relationship that countries and communities around the world have today. It is also used to describe our social, political, and cultural interdependence.

2 An example of global transformation is fast food. Different countries transform a food based on the local ingredients that are available.

⌒ LISTENING FOR TONE OF VOICE

Make sure that students understand the following vocabulary: *tone of voice, disbelief, degree, mild, stress*.

Answers to step 2 (Student's Book page 145)

1 Place: Kuwait
Reaction: strong surprise

2 Place: Japan
Reaction: mild surprise

3 Place: Los Angeles
Reaction: mild surprise

4 Place: Thailand
Reaction: strong surprise

2 AMERICAN VOICES: Adam, María, Lindsay, and Chander (Student's Book pages 146–149)

BEFORE THE INTERVIEWS

SHARING YOUR KNOWLEDGE

Allow students time to discuss what they know about practices related to health and exercise: *karate, shiatsu massage, yoga, tai chi, salsa, acupuncture, tango,* and *chiropractic*. Because these practices are multicultural, it is likely that different students in the class will know different information about them, depending on their backgrounds. For example, karate is a Japanese martial art, but its earliest origins were in Chinese martial arts. This is an ideal time to allow students to demonstrate what they know about these topics. Also make sure the following question is discussed in preparation for the interviews and lecture: Why do you think these activities have become popular in many countries?

INTERVIEW WITH ADAM AND MARIA: *Two health practices*

Look at the pictures of Adam and María and read aloud the items in the vocabulary box on page 147.

RETELLING WHAT YOU HAVE HEARD

Answers to step 2 (Student's Book page 147)

Practice	Place of origin	How it is used differently in the United States than in its place of origin
acupuncture	Asia orig. 21,000 yrs ago	in Asia: ancient medical practice in U.S.: lux, not gen paid for by insurance
yoga	India orig. > 2,000 yrs ago	in India: trad relig prac → Hindu religion In U.S.: exercise

INTERVIEW WITH LINDSAY AND CHANDER: *Cars and food*

Look at the pictures of Lindsay and Chander and read aloud the vocabulary in the box on page 148.

⌒ RETELLING WHAT YOU HAVE HEARD

Answers to step 2 (Student's Book page 148)

Item	Place of origin	How it is used differently in the United States than in its place of origin
car (Volkswagen)	Germany	in Germany: cars often have manual trans in U.S.: ppl like automatics – cars often made with bigger engines
food (Indian)	India	in India: trad foods incl hot/strong spices – Amers not used to in U.S.: less rice served – sometimes chef adds mayo/sour cream

AFTER THE INTERVIEWS

DEVELOPING CONVERSATIONS ABOUT A TOPIC

Explain that developing a conversation about a particular topic is a good way for students to practice the vocabulary they have learned as well as to contribute their own perspective on the topic.

The topics in these conversation starters are acupuncture, which could lead to a discussion of other alternative treatments; yoga, which could lead to a discussion of other forms of exercise and relaxation; cars, which could lead to a discussion of other products imported from abroad; and food, which could lead to a discussion of different people's preferences for foreign cuisine.

3 IN YOUR OWN VOICE (Student's Book pages 150–151)

SHARING YOUR KNOWLEDGE

This interactive activity allows for the sharing of a lot of interesting information in an oral format. The playful nature of the activity also allows students to express degrees of surprise or disbelief, as learned in the activity in "Getting Started."

Review the rules with students before they begin the activity. There are two questions for each item. The first question asks students to identify the item in question, for which students can assign one point for each correct response. The second question is a true/false question. Answers for each item are provided on pages 158 and 159 of the Student's Book.

4 ACADEMIC LISTENING AND NOTE TAKING: The Globalization of American Slang (Student's Book pages 152–157)

BEFORE THE LECTURE

BUILDING VOCABULARY

> Review the correct answers and pronunciation of the slang terms and allow students to discuss other American slang expressions that they know.

Answers to step 1 (Student's Book page 152)

1 awesome
2 see ya
3 stuff
4 clueless
5 guy
6 chill out
7 beat
8 whatever
9 way to go
10 a big deal

🎧 NOTE TAKING: LISTENING FOR RESTATEMENTS

Answers to steps 1 and 2 (Student's Book page 153)

1 Slang is, and I'm quoting a dictionary here, "a type of language used especially in speech among particular *speech communities*," that is, groups of people who use language in a particular way that is acceptable to all of them.

2 Slang is tremendously popular among young people, because it's all about "*what's happening now.*" That means that it evolves, or in other words, adapts and changes rapidly.

3 This way of speaking is very attractive: it's creative and cool, as I mentioned, and it's very *youth-oriented*, meaning that it appeals to young people.

4 Young people around the world hear *celebrities*, you know, famous actors or singers, speaking or singing American slang.

5 In the last quarter century, this word has *invaded every corner of the English-speaking world*. . . . I mean, you hear it almost everywhere you go.

LECTURE, PART ONE: What Is American Slang?

GUESSING VOCABULARY FROM CONTEXT

Answers to step 2 (Student's Book page 153)

c	1
a	2
b	3
d	4

🎧 NOTE TAKING: COMBINING THE SKILLS

Review the skills that students have learned in this book. Then have students take notes during the lecture on their own paper with no support.

Encourage students to look critically at their notes and identify areas where they have made a lot of improvement or some improvement and areas where they need to improve more. If possible, have students share and/or rewrite the notes they have taken, either in pairs or in small groups.

LECTURE, PART TWO: Why American Slang Travels the Globe

GUESSING VOCABULARY FROM CONTEXT

Answers to step 2 (Student's Book page 155)

c	**1**
e	**2**
d	**3**
f	**4**
a	**5**
b	**6**

🎧 NOTE TAKING: COMBINING THE SKILLS

Supervise students as they take notes on their own paper using the skills they learned in this book and reviewed on page 154. Then have them reorganize and rewrite their notes. Ask students to exchange their notes with a partner and work together to evaluate each other's work, focusing especially on the skills the students have mastered.

AFTER THE LECTURE

UNDERSTANDING HUMOR ABOUT THE TOPIC

The last activity in the book allows students to share their understanding of humorists' comments on American slang. If the classroom configuration allows, you could divide the class into three groups and have each group describe a different cartoon.

Another activity that encourages interaction is to do this exercise having students cover the two cartoons that they themselves are not describing. Their task is to draw the cartoon according to their classmate's description. This activity requires serious and active listening and is an engaging way of treating humorous topics.

Chapter 10 Lecture Quiz

See the Lecture Quiz section at the back of this Teacher's Manual for a photocopiable quiz on the lecture for Chapter 10. Quiz answers can be found on page 132.

Additional Ideas for Unit 5

Key topics in this unit are: American innovations in different areas of life, such as digital technology, sports, and movies; American musical genres, particularly blues and country; and global transformations, including the way American slang travels the globe.

1 Have students find examples of innovators, meaning the people who are responsible for the innovations that affect our lives.

2 Ask students to listen online, on CDs, or on the radio, to blues and country music. Ask them to identify the elements that they have learned about in this unit.

3 Have students research recipes of foods from different countries or prepare a dish from another country that they can share with classmates. Ask them to make a list of ingredients that are difficult or impossible to find in your area. Alternatively, have students bring in hard-to-find ingredients (such as spices) from their home country to show to the class.

4 Ask students to imagine life without the following innovations that have shaped contemporary life: the Internet, TV, CDs, cell phones, iPods, microwave ovens, and so on. How difficult would it be for students to spend one week without digital technology?

5 Have students watch a segment of *Waking Life*, a groundbreaking 2001 animated film featuring rotoscoping.

6 Have the class compile a dictionary of slang terms. Each student should contribute all the terms they know.

Listening Script

Listening Script

Narrator: *Academic Listening Encounters: American Studies*
Listening, Note Taking, and Discussion
by Kim Sanabria and Carlos Sanabria
Series editor: Bernard Seal
Published by Cambridge University Press
This audio program contains the listening material for the *Academic Listening Encounters: American Studies* Student's Book. This recording is copyright.

1

Narrator: CD 1
Chapter 1, The Foundations of Government
Page 3
Previewing the topic, Step 2

Man: Hey, did you ever take a close look at the back of a one-dollar bill?

Woman: No, not really. Is there something special about it?

Man: Well, yeah. See, it has some really interesting symbols on it.

Woman: Let me see. Hmmm. The two circles . . . aren't they the two sides of the Great Seal?

Man: That's right. And see the pyramid in the circle on the left? It means that America has a strong foundation. And look on the bottom. You see the number 1776 in Roman numerals? That's the year the United States became an independent country. And there are some symbols in the other circle, too.

Woman: Let me get a closer look. There's a bird . . .

Man: Yeah, that's the bald eagle. It's the national symbol of the United States.

Woman: And some writing in Latin . . .

Man: Uh-huh, *e pluribus unum*. That means "Out of many, one." It means that the United States is made up of many states and many people, but it's still one nation, see?

Woman: Yeah, sure. What about the stars above the eagle's head? What do they mean?

Man: They're symbols for the original 13 states. And see, there are other groups of 13 in the Great Seal, too. Like the pyramid has 13 steps.

Woman: Wow. I had no idea a one-dollar bill was so full of meaning.

Man: I know. It's really interesting. Now I'm going to try to find out what some of the other symbols mean.

Narrator: Now complete the steps in your book.

Narrator: Chapter 1, The Foundations of Government
Page 6
Listening for different ways of saying *yes* and *no*, Step 2

Interviewer: I'd like to ask all of you some questions about voting. Manuel, you first: Do you vote?

Manuel: Well, not usually. I'm always too busy on Election Day. I can never seem to get to the polls.

Interviewer: Why is that? The polls are open from six in the morning until nine at night.

Manuel: Yes, but it's still not convenient for a lot of people. I didn't vote for President while I was in college because I had too much to do. Then the next election, I had a really crazy day and I just couldn't make it. I don't really understand how in this great democracy people have to work on Election Day. I think we should get a national holiday, like they do in a lot of other countries, so that we can vote.

Interviewer: That's an interesting suggestion. Now what about you Mary, do you vote?

Mary: Sure.

Interviewer: And . . . why?

Mary: It's important for citizens to vote because it gives you a voice, and a feeling that you have the power to make a difference. When you vote, you get to say who you feel is the best candidate, who can help more in dealing with the country's problems.

Interviewer: And do you believe your vote can really make a difference?

Mary: Absolutely! I mean, if millions of people vote for what they believe, they have a lot of power! I disagree with Manuel. If people really want to vote, they can find time on Election Day to do it.

Interviewer: Kelly, what about you? Do you vote?

Kelly: Yeah, I do. I voted as soon as I turned 18. Frankly, I can't understand people who don't bother to vote. Let's say only 50 percent of the population votes, and then the President wins by only a few votes. That's what happened in the 2000 election. So basically, the President was elected by only 25 percent of all the people in the country. That's terrible! I think voting is a civic duty and it should be compulsory. I read that in 34 countries voting is an obligation, that it's required by law.

Interviewer: And you, Ralph, do you vote?

Ralph: Nah, I haven't recently. I feel like even if I do vote, nothing ever changes. It doesn't seem to make any difference who's in power. Actually, I don't trust most politicians. When they run for office, they make a lot of promises, but then they don't keep them.

Narrator: Now complete the steps in your book.

Narrator: Chapter 1, The Foundations of Government
Page 8
Listening for main ideas in an interview, Step 2

Interviewer: So Bob, why do you think so few Americans vote?

Bob: Well, some people don't think it will make any difference. It is true that we have two political parties – Republicans and Democrats – but today, those parties are very similar. A lot of people feel there is no real choice, so they feel like their vote isn't meaningful.

Interviewer: But you vote, don't you?

Bob: Yes, I certainly do! I think people should vote, because we have to try to make some changes in this country.

Interviewer: What kind of changes? I mean, what are some issues that you think are important today?

Bob: Let's see . . . Well, one is immigration. This is something that people feel very strongly about – and we need to express our opinion. Another issue is homelessness. I mean, this is one of the richest countries in the world, but there are still people sleeping on the streets.

Interviewer: Yeah, those are definitely big concerns for a lot of people.

Bob: And most people my age are also talking about health care – that's another really big issue. There are millions of people without health insurance in the United States.

Interviewer: I see why you think it's important to vote.

Bob: Yes, it is very important, because we live in a democracy, and we need to elect representatives who share our concerns.

Narrator: Now complete the steps in your book.

Narrator: Chapter 1, The Foundations of Government
Page 11
Listening for the plan of a lecture, Step 2

Edward Sullivan: Hi. Welcome to you all. My name is Ed Sullivan, and I was an elected official in New York State for many years. Before that, I also taught English for about 15 years. And you know, whenever I speak to students, I always get a lot of questions about the basic structure of the federal government. So what I'm going to do today is give you an overview of how the government is organized, and that way, you can start to understand how it works. First, I'll introduce the three branches of government. And I'll be using this chart here on the board to help you understand.

And then, after that, I'll explain the system of checks and balances.

Narrator: Now complete the steps in your book.

**Narrator: Chapter 1, The Foundations of Government
Page 14
Note taking: Using information the lecturer puts on the board, Step 1**

Edward Sullivan: Hi. Welcome to you all. My name is Ed Sullivan, and I was an elected official in New York State for many years. Before that, I also taught English for about 15 years. And you know, whenever I speak to students, I always get a lot of questions about the basic structure of the federal government. So what I'm going to do today is give you an overview of how the government is organized, and that way, you can start to understand how it works. First, I'll introduce the three branches of government. And I'll be using this chart here on the board to help you understand. And then, after that, I'll explain the system of checks and balances.

All right, now, as you can see on the board, the U.S. government has three branches, or parts, called legislative, executive, and judicial. So let me start with the legislative branch, which makes the laws. So here on the left, where it says "responsibilities," I'm writing "makes laws." OK. In the U.S., the legislative branch of government is called Congress. And Congress actually has two parts, or houses: the Senate and the House of Representatives. Members of the Senate are called Senators, and members of the House are called Representatives. Have you got that? OK.

Good. So now let me give you a few more details about Congress. Each state has two Senators, and since there are 50 states, there are exactly 100 senators. On the other hand, the House of Representatives has 435 members. And that's because the number of

representatives from each state depends on the size of the state's population. Obviously, states with larger populations, like California, have more representatives.

All right. The next branch of government I want to describe is the executive branch, which executes, or approves, the laws that Congress makes. And who has that job? The President. Actually the President has many responsibilities, but the most important one is the power to approve laws. Now besides the President, the executive branch also includes the Vice President and the heads of government departments, who are called secretaries – you know, Secretary of State, Secretary of Defense, Secretary of Education, and so on.

Finally there's the judicial branch. *Judicial* is related to the word *judge*. Now, there are three levels of courts in the United States: city, state, and federal. But when we talk about the judicial branch of the federal government, we're usually talking about the Supreme Court, which is the highest court in the land. The Supreme Court has nine members, called justices, and their job is to interpret the laws passed by Congress, in other words, to decide if a law is constitutional or not.

Narrator: Now complete the steps in your book.

**Narrator: Chapter 1, The Foundations of Government
Page 14
Note taking: Taking good lecture notes, Step 1**

Edward Sullivan: OK. Now why do you think the federal government is divided this way? Well, the Founding Fathers, meaning the men who wrote the Constitution, wanted to avoid a dictatorship. They didn't want one person or one branch to have too much power, and to make sure this didn't happen, they invented a system of "checks and balances." Checks and balances means that the three branches of government have separate responsibilities, but they also have the power to check, or limit, each other's actions.

Let me give you some examples of how checks and balances work. The way Supreme Court justices are chosen is a good example. Supreme Court justices aren't elected. They're chosen by the President. But the Senate has the power to approve or disapprove of the President's choice. The Senate, in this case, can check the President's power to choose Supreme Court justices.

Here's another example. Let's suppose Congress passes a law, but the President doesn't want to approve it. If that happens, the Constitution gives the President the power to veto it – in other words, he can decide not to sign it. And according to the Constitution, a law doesn't become a law until the President signs it. So in this case, the President is checking the power of Congress.

Let me give you a third example. Suppose Congress passes a law and the President signs it. Is that the end of the process? Usually yes, but sometimes no. Sometimes someone challenges the constitutionality of a law. It can be a private citizen or a corporation or a city government who says a law is wrong or unfair because it goes against the Constitution. Most cases like that will be heard in a lower-level court. But the Supreme Court has the final authority to decide if the law – which was passed by Congress and signed by the President, remember – is either constitutional or unconstitutional. So this is an example of the Supreme Court checking and balancing both of the other branches.

So I hope that now you have a basic understanding of the three branches of the U.S. government and how these branches control each other through the system of checks and balances.

Narrator: Now complete the steps in your book.

Narrator: Chapter 2, Constitutional Issues Today
Page 17
Understanding numbers, dates, and time expressions, Step 2

Narrator: One.
Man: The United States declared its independence from Britain on July 4, 1776.

Narrator: Two.
Man: The Constitution was adopted in 1789.

Narrator: Three.
Man: The Bill of Rights became part of the Constitution in 1791.

Narrator: Four.
Actor: The American Civil War took place between 1861 and 1865.

Narrator: Five.
Man: The Thirteenth Amendment ended slavery in 1865.

Narrator: Six.
Man: The Fifteenth Amendment gave African-American men the right to vote in 1870.

Narrator: Seven.
Man: From 1787 to 1920, only men had the right to vote.

Narrator: Eight.
Man: In 1920, the Nineteenth Amendment gave women the right to vote.

Narrator: Nine.
Man: On July 1, 1971, the Twenty-sixth Amendment lowered the voting age to 18.

Narrator: Now complete the steps in your book.

Narrator: Chapter 2, Constitutional Issues Today
Page 21
Listening for specific information, Step 2

Interviewer: Hi, Magda. Can you tell me about a constitutional right that's especially important to you?

Magda: Yes! Freedom of speech – and of course that includes the freedom to express yourself in words or in any other way, even if people don't agree with you. That's really important to me in my work as an artist.

Interviewer: What kind of art do you do?

Magda: I'm a photographer, and as a photographer, I believe censorship is wrong. Art is a powerful way of expressing ideas, and ideas can be very controversial. But I don't think anyone has the right to tell people what they can see.

Interviewer: Does that ever happen?

Magda: Yeah, it happens all the time! For example, the government has always censored violent photographs during wartime. And then just a few years ago, there was an exhibit called "Sensation" in a museum in New York, and there were paintings and sculptures that showed famous religious figures in ways that were very offensive to some people.

Interviewer: So what happened?

Magda: Well, the mayor tried to close the exhibit!

Interviewer: Didn't you agree with that?

Madga: No, of course not! Look, even if you personally disagree with the message of a piece of art, you have to allow artists the freedom to express themselves. That's our constitutional right!

Interviewer: Well, now let me turn to you, Hang, and ask you the same question, if there's a constitutional right that's especially important for you.

Hang: Well, recently I've really come to value the fact that in the United States, we have freedom of assembly. This includes the right to demonstrate and complain and demand change. The First Amendment gives us that right.

Interviewer: Did something happen to make you start thinking about this?

Hang: Yes, there was a big demonstration at my college. The students wanted the university to stop buying products from companies that use child labor. See, a lot of university products, like hats and T-shirts, are made in countries that allow children to work in factories.

Interviewer: And what happened after the demonstration?

Hang: Well, the university changed its policy. So you see, our protests were very effective.

Narrator: Now complete the steps in your book.

Narrator: Chapter 2, Constitutional Issues Today
Page 22
Listening for specific information, Step 2

Interviewer: Gloria, let's turn to you now. Can you identify an important constitutional right?

Gloria: Well, the right to bear arms, you know, to own a gun, is important for me. I know this is very controversial, and a lot of people disagree with me, but I believe the Second Amendment gives us that right.

Interviewer: Why do people disagree with you?

Gloria: Well, the words of the Second Amendment aren't exactly clear. Some people think it means that only the police or soldiers have the right to have guns. But I don't think that's right.

Interviewer: But if everyone has the right to own a gun, aren't you worried that some people will use them for the wrong reasons?

Gloria: Well, yeah, of course, but . . . look, there are two groups of people who own guns. One is criminals . . . and they will own guns anyway, whether it's legal or not! And the second group is responsible citizens who own guns for good reasons.

Interviewer: What are those reasons?

Gloria: Well, some people have guns for sports, like hunting or target shooting, and others have guns for self-protection.

Interviewer: Self-protection? Do you think that's really necessary?

Gloria: Yes! The police can't be everywhere to protect people, so store owners and homeowners in some areas might feel they need a gun to protect themselves.

Narrator: Now complete the steps in your book.

Narrator: Chapter 2, Constitutional Issues Today
Page 26
Note taking: Listening for main ideas and supporting details, Step 2

Narrator: Excerpt 1.

Marcella Bencivenni: What does it mean to have freedom of religion? Basically it means two things: First, Americans are free to practice their religion without interference from the government, and second, there is no national religion. Now this freedom affects Americans in many ways. For instance, an employer can't hire you or fire you just because he likes or doesn't like your religion. And freedom of religion even includes how you dress. What I mean is, Americans are free to wear any kind of religious clothing they prefer.

Narrator: Excerpt 2.

Marcella Bencivenni: All right. Now, the next freedom listed in the First Amendment is maybe the most famous one, because it's the one that all of us practice every single day, and that's freedom of speech. What does that mean, exactly? Basically, it means you're free to talk openly about your ideas, even if other people disagree with them. You're also free to read or listen to other people's ideas. But in addition, freedom of speech includes what we call "symbolic speech" – like wearing the clothes you like. In fact, the courts have said that freedom of speech includes *all* forms of expression,

meaning words, pictures, music, even the way you wear your hair!

Narrator: Now complete the steps in your book.

Narrator: Chapter 2, Constitutional Issues Today
Page 28
Note taking: Using symbols and abbreviations, Step 3

Marcella Bencivenni: Today's lecture is about the First Amendment to the U.S. Constitution, which for many Americans is probably the most important part of the Bill of Rights, because it affects the way we live every day. I'll begin with an overview of the five freedoms in the First Amendment, and after that, in the second part of my talk, I'll tell you about some cases that will show you why the First Amendment is so controversial.

So, now the First Amendment guarantees American citizens five basic freedoms: freedom of religion, speech, press, assembly, and petition. What does it mean to have freedom of religion? Basically it means two things: First, Americans are free to practice their religion without interference from the government, and second, there is no national religion. Now this freedom affects Americans in many ways. For instance, an employer can't hire you or fire you just because he likes or doesn't like your religion. And freedom of religion even includes how you dress. What I mean is, Americans are free to wear any kind of religious clothing they prefer. For example, some religions require people to cover their heads all the time, while others require people to take their hats *off*, for example, in church. Both of these forms of expression are legal.

All right. Now, the next freedom listed in the First Amendment is maybe the most famous one, because it's the one that all of us practice every single day, and that's freedom of speech. What does that mean, exactly? Basically, it means you're free to talk openly about your ideas, even if other people disagree with them. You're also free to read or listen to other people's ideas. But in addition, freedom of speech includes what we call "symbolic speech" – like wearing the clothes you like. In fact, the courts have said that freedom of speech includes *all* forms of expression, meaning words, pictures, music, even the way you wear your hair!

The third freedom, freedom of the press, means the freedom that books, newspapers, magazines, and today, also the Internet, have to freely publish different ideas and opinions. Let's say you open a magazine, and you see a cartoon making a joke about the President. You might ask yourself: Is that legal? And the answer is yes. It's also perfectly legal for a journalist to write an article criticizing the government. You can open the newspaper any day and find articles that criticize the government for, oh, let's see, raising taxes or not protecting the environment, or, well of course, military activities in other countries. Journalists are free to agree or disagree with these actions and express their opinions without fear.

The First Amendment lists two other freedoms as well: freedom of assembly and freedom of petition. Freedom of assembly means, very simply, the right to meet in groups. When students participate in demonstrations on college campuses, for example, they are using their right of assembly and the right of free speech at the same time.

And the fifth and last freedom is freedom of petition, which means citizens have the right to ask the government to change laws or change policies. In other words, it means that citizens can complain about the government's actions.

I've listed these five freedoms separately, but in real life, we often use the term "freedom of expression" to talk about all of them. Freedom of expression means the right that Americans have to express

their views in any form they prefer, for example, by speaking, writing a letter to their senator, demonstrating in the streets, writing a song, or painting a picture.

Narrator: Now complete the steps in your book.

Narrator: Chapter 2, Constitutional Issues Today
Page 30
Note taking: Using a map to organize your notes, Step 3

Marcella Bencivenni: Perhaps you're wondering: Does the First Amendment mean Americans are completely free to say and do whatever they want? And of course the answer is no. There are limits, but trying to decide where and what they are can be very controversial. Let's look at the kinds of questions that our courts deal with all the time.

The first question is: What are the limits of free speech? You see, in practice, there are some restrictions. For example, it's never legal to publish lies about people. But should it be legal to burn the U.S. flag as a form of criticism against the government? Some people say yes because the First Amendment guarantees free expression. But many other people disagree. They think flag burning is unpatriotic and insults the government. You might be surprised to hear that the Supreme Court has ruled that flag burning is legal, but this is very controversial.

Here's another question. Should children be allowed to bring cell phones to school? Many teachers and principals say no, because cell phones make noise in class, and they've tried to forbid cell phones or take them away from children. However, many parents say they need to have a way to get in touch with their children, and they also say that using a cell phone is a form of free speech.

Let's look at another controversial question that often comes up: What does freedom of religion actually mean, in practice? For example, do you think children should have the right to say prayers in public schools? Some people say yes because the First Amendment guarantees freedom of religion, right? But other people say no because the First Amendment also says there cannot be any national religion. And since public schools are open to children of all religions, these people believe there shouldn't be any religious activities in these schools. Basically, the courts have said that students can pray at school privately, but they can't do it during class time, and the school or the teachers cannot organize or encourage any kind of religious activity.

So to conclude what I've been saying, the freedoms promised in the Bill of Rights can be very controversial.

Narrator: Now complete the steps in your book.

3

Narrator: Chapter 3, The Origins of Diversity Page 35
Listening for numerical information, Step 2

Woman: Around 1820, immigration to the United States began to rise quickly. It continued to climb through the first decade of the twentieth century, when immigration figures became very high.

Woman: Immigration began to fall around 1910. It continued falling after World War I began in Europe in 1914. When the United States entered the War in 1917, immigration declined even more.

Woman: Laws passed in the 1920s limited immigration even more.

Woman: During the Great Depression, beginning in 1929, it was not easy to get a job in America, and immigration decreased to its lowest point.

Woman: Immigration increased quickly after World War II. Today, at the beginning of the twenty-first century, it's climbing rapidly again. Immigration figures today are higher than they've ever been.

Narrator: Now complete the steps in your book.

Narrator: Chapter 3, The Origins of Diversity Page 39
Answering true/false questions, Step 2

Interviewer: Patrick, where did your family come from originally?

Patrick: Ireland. My grandparents both came from the same small village in Ireland. First, my grandfather came over in the 1860s, and then as soon as he got a job, my grandmother came, too. You know, that was the big thing back then – come to America! Anyway, after my grandparents, all the brothers and sisters and all the cousins came, too.

Interviewer: The whole family?

Patrick: Yeah. See, in Ireland they would get letters from America saying that there were jobs here. It was so, so poor over there. I'm talking about the mid- to late nineteenth century . . . and there had been a potato famine there, you know, in 1848. There was just no food, and people were desperate. About a million people died, can you imagine? But in America, there was opportunity. So the Irish started coming over in massive numbers.

Interviewer: What was life like for them here?

Patrick: Well, they stuck together. The relatives helped the other relatives get jobs. And they had to share their apartments, so you know, it wasn't always so easy. And they were really poor. I mean, I think a lot of people arrived with less than $50 in their pockets. So they depended on each other to survive.

Interviewer: Hmm.

Patrick: And then they were Catholic. That set them apart. I've heard there was a lot of prejudice against them because they had different religious beliefs. But on the other hand, they made a lot of contributions to society.

Interviewer: What kind of contributions did they make?

Patrick: Well, they got involved in city politics. And they worked hard, in factories and in the police force. And a lot of them were firefighters. And, they cared for their communities and their families. Because one thing that's very important to the Irish is family. My father came from a big family – there were ten boys and one girl. That's one thing about the Irish. Lots of big families!

Narrator: Now complete the steps in your book.

Narrator: Chapter 3, The Origins of Diversity Page 40
Listening for specific information, Step 2

Interviewer: Eunice and John, your families both came to the U.S. in the early 1900s. Could you tell me their stories? Eunice, would you begin?

Eunice: Well, my family is Jewish, and they came from Russia. And for a lot of Jews, you know, there was always a fear of religious persecution. Thousands of Jews were killed in Russia. But in America, there was freedom to practice our religion.

Interviewer: So they came for religious freedom.

Eunice: But it wasn't only for religion, it was political freedom, too. Because in Russia at that time, if you criticized the government, you'd end up in jail! And then the third reason they came here was for the economic opportunities. They wanted the chance to have better jobs and to live more comfortably, and to make a better life for their children. That's what happened to my grandparents.

Interviewer: Was it difficult for them in the United States?

Eunice: Yes, because they were very poor. I mean, they had almost no money at all. My mother used to talk about what it was like

as a child. You know what the kids got for a gift? An orange! And this was so valued, this piece of fruit. But life was difficult in other ways, too. In the United States, it was harder to keep the family close. I think that was probably the hardest thing of all.

Interviewer: And John, what about your family?

John: Well, my family's Italian. My grandparents came from a small village in the south of Italy where my grandfather's family had all been fishermen . . . and life was very hard for them, too, because the economy was bad, and they couldn't make a living.

Interviewer: Was it hard for them to leave Italy?

John: Well, it wasn't easy. The trip alone was a nightmare. I heard a lot of people died on the boat. And when they finally arrived, they were almost penniless, and of course they didn't speak the language.

Interviewer: What happened after they arrived?

John: Let's see, my grandfather got a job in a factory. My grandmother took care of the children, and she was also a midwife. They had nine kids! And my father was the youngest one of those nine kids.

Interviewer: Wow, that was a big family!

John: Yes, it was. And times were pretty tough because later, when my parents were born – it was the 1930s, the time of the Depression. But my father was a good student, and he ended up getting a scholarship to college. My father was the first one in his family to graduate from college. That gave him a lot more opportunities.

Interviewer: You sound very proud of him.

John: I am. You know, as I look back on it, I see that my family struggled hard to make a better life in this country. And there was, like, a kind of a feeling of living in two different worlds because they spoke two languages and had two cultures. But they were proud of it, and I am, too.

Narrator: Now complete the steps in your book.

Narrator: One.

Gerald Meyer: The four major groups that immigrated to the U.S. during this time were the Germans, the Irish, the Jews from Russia, and the Italians. Of course, there were many other immigrants – for instance, from Poland, Greece, Hungary, China, and Mexico.

Narrator: Two.

Gerald Meyer: And all of them met with a lot of prejudice in this country. And by prejudice, I mean that Americans did things like calling them cruel names or refusing to let them rent an apartment or refusing to give them a job.

Narrator: Three.

Gerald Meyer: Americans were worried about the size and diversity of the new foreign population. You have to remember that millions of immigrants arrived during this time, in fact, almost 30 million of them.

Narrator: Four.

Gerald Meyer: Most people in the United States were Protestants, and they were often prejudiced against the Catholics, and also against the Jews. One reason for this was that the immigrants' religious practices and traditions seemed strange to them.

Narrator: Five.

Gerald Meyer: The Irish, on the other hand, helped build the infrastructure of many American cities – in other words, the canals, the bridges, the railroads, the seaports, and the roads.

Narrator: Now complete the steps in your book.

Gerald Meyer: Good morning, everyone. Today I want to talk to you about the experience of immigrants who came to the United States from the middle of the nineteenth to the beginning of the twentieth centuries, from, oh, about 1840 to about 1917. As you know, there was a strong prejudice against these early immigrants, but even so, these groups were able to make important and lasting contributions to American society. So, for the next few minutes I'm going to discuss both of these parts of the immigrant experience: the prejudice as well as the contributions.

Now just to remind you, the four major groups that immigrated to the U.S. during this time were the Germans, the Irish, the Jews from Russia, and the Italians. Of course, there were many other immigrants – for instance, from Poland, Greece, Hungary, China, and Mexico. And all of them met with a lot of prejudice in this country. And by prejudice, I mean that Americans did things like calling them cruel names or refusing to let them rent an apartment or refusing to give them a job. So now, what were some of the reasons for this?

Well, to begin with, Americans were worried about the size and diversity of the new foreign population. You have to remember that millions of immigrants arrived during this time, in fact, almost 30 million of them. And most of them crowded into cities in the eastern and northern parts of the United States. I'm sure it was frightening for many Americans to see so many strangers moving into their cities. But there were other reasons for the prejudice against immigrants, too.

Many immigrants faced prejudice because they had different religious beliefs. Most people in the United States were Protestants, and they were often prejudiced against the Catholics, and also against the Jews. One reason for this was that the immigrants' religious practices and traditions seemed strange to them. Then, third, there was prejudice against new immigrants who spoke different languages and had unfamiliar customs: different foods, different clothes, things like that. Also, many Americans were afraid that the immigrants wouldn't share their democratic values. For example, there was also a lot of prejudice against the Germans around the time of the First World War because the United States was fighting against Germany, and people thought Germans living in America might be unpatriotic.

And finally, many Americans were afraid that with all these immigrants coming over, they would lose their jobs . . . that the immigrants would work for less money than they would. And so, for all these reasons, immigrants were seen as a threat to the American way of life.

Narrator: Now complete the steps in your book.

Narrator: Chapter 3, The Origins of Diversity
Page 48
Note taking: Organizing your notes in columns, Step 2

Gerald Meyer: What you have to remember is that this time . . . well, it was a time of great expansion in America. Cities and industries were growing, and a lot of people were moving west, so the country needed a large number of new workers. A lot of these new workers were immigrants who made many important and lasting contributions to the development of the country.

For example, many Germans became farmers. They were good at farming and made important improvements to U.S. farming methods. In addition, Germans also worked as tailors, bakers, and butchers. The Irish, on the other hand, helped build the infrastructure of many American cities – in other words,

the canals, the bridges, the railroads, the seaports, and the roads. Many were skilled workers, like plumbers, and others were unskilled factory workers.

The Jews – who were mostly from Russia at this time – and the Italians – also made important contributions to the nation. For example, as the years went by, many Jews became involved in popular music and in entertainment. They were also important to the development of American education and science. Many also worked in the clothing industry. The Italians, like the Irish, were important in the construction industry and in the building of roads, canals, bridges, buildings, and railroads.

In the end, there's no doubt that all these immigrants made important contributions to the economy and culture of the United States. The reason this country is so well known as a country of immigrants is because of all the languages, foods, music, religions, beliefs, and lifestyles that all these different people brought with them.

Narrator: Now complete the steps in your book.

Narrator: Chapter 4, Diversity in Today's United States
Page 51
Listening for percentages and fractions, Step 3

Man: Chart 1 shows immigration to the United States between 1901 and 1940. At this time, 79 percent of immigrants came from Europe, 6 percent came from Latin America, and 4 percent came from Asia. Eleven percent came from other places.

Man: Chart 2 shows immigration to the United States between 1941 and 1980. During this period, 34 percent – or about one-third of all immigrants – came from Europe, another 34 percent came from Latin

America, and 19 percent came from Asia. Thirteen percent came from other places.

Man: Chart 3 shows immigration to the United States between 1981 and 2000. Forty-seven percent – almost half of all immigrants – came from Latin America, and 34 percent came from Asia. Only 13 percent came from Europe, and 6 percent came from other places.

Narrator: Now complete the steps in your book.

Narrator: Chapter 4, Diversity in Today's United States
Page 54
Listening for specific information, Step 2

Interviewer: Agustín, where are you from, and how long have you been in the U.S.?

Agustín: I'm from Mexico. I've been here . . . oh, over 20 years now.

Interviewer: And why did you come?

Agustín: Well, the reason I came, like most Mexicans, I suppose, was to work. In my country there aren't enough jobs. It's hard to make a living.

Interviewer: And what was your biggest difficulty when you came here?

Agustín: The hardest thing for me at first was that I didn't know anyone, except for my brother. I was lucky that he helped me a lot. He sent me money, he gave me a place to live, and he helped me find a job.

Interviewer: And how are you doing now?

Agustín: I'm doing well. When I first came, I was washing dishes, but I didn't want to get stuck doing that. Now I work in a food store, and I work directly with people.

Interviewer: And don't you miss your family in Mexico?

Agustín: Sure, but we're often in contact. I always send money and presents back home.

Interviewer: Nadezhda, what about you? Where were you born, and how long have you been in the U.S.?

Nadezhda: I was born in Russia, and I've been here about four years.

Interviewer: And why did you come?

Nadezhda: Well, mainly because of my children. In the United States, I feel that I can build a better life for them, a rich life with many possibilities.

Interviewer: What kind of possibilities?

Nadezhda: Education. There are more educational opportunities in America. I dream of giving my kids an excellent education. I think that's the most important goal in life.

Interviewer: Was it hard to leave Russia?

Nadezhda: Yes, it was, because I love my country. And, well, my mother is still there, and it was very difficult for me to leave her. But I made a sacrifice for my children. And we are doing well. In fact, I just became a citizen!

Interviewer: Congratulations, Nadezhda! OK, now, Chao . . . you're from . . .

Chao: China.

Interviewer: And how long have you been here, and why did you come?

Chao: I've been here for 10 years. I came for two reasons. The first reason was to join my family. I was living with my aunt in China. My parents and my grandparents were in the U.S., and I wanted to be with them. And the second reason was to study. I want to become a physician's assistant. It's easier to get that kind of training in the U.S.

Interviewer: Have you had any difficulties?

Chao: Well, it's hard to work and study at the same time. And then it was also difficult to learn English. At home we speak Chinese – only Chinese. And at work – I work in a tofu factory – I only speak Chinese there, too. It's hard, but I love living in America, because you can meet people from all over the world, and I'm studying to make my dream come true.

Narrator: Now complete the steps in your book.

Narrator: **Chapter 4, Diversity in Today's United States**
Page 55
Listening for specific information, Step 2

Interviewer: Alvin, your family is from Puerto Rico, right?

Alvin: Yeah, but I grew up in the States.

Interviewer: OK, so, let me ask you: Do you think you're American or Puerto Rican?

Alvin: Let's put it this way: I think I'm a hybrid, because I'm a combination of two cultures. I'm American on the outside, but I'm Puerto Rican inside.

Interviewer: How do you mean?

Alvin: Well, see, whenever I'm at home, we always speak Spanish. We listen to Latin music, we eat Puerto Rican food . . . You know, it doesn't feel at all American. But whenever I step outside the door, I step into a different world where they speak English and have a completely different culture. So I'm constantly going back and forth between the two cultures.

Interviewer: That's a good way to explain it, Alvin, thanks. Now, Minsoo . . . I know you're from Korea, right?

Minsoo: Yes. I've lived here for about five years. I came here because there are a lot more opportunities for women here.

Interviewer: Your English is very good. Do you speak it at home?

Minsoo: No, I only speak Korean. It's easier to express myself. I only speak English at work and in college.

Interviewer: Is it difficult for you to speak English?

Minsoo: No, not really. The only time it's hard is when . . . well, in school, for instance, the professor expects us to speak in front of everyone else. I'm not used to giving my opinion in class. In Korea, students are supposed to take notes and do their homework, not talk in class all the time!

Interviewer: Would you say you're more Korean, or more American?

Minsoo: I think half and half. 50-50. I have my Korean culture, but I'm absorbing American culture fast.

Interviewer: And Abdoul-Aziz, what about you? You're originally from . . .

Abdoul-Aziz: Niger. That's where I grew up. I came here as an adult.

Interviewer: And, you speak . . .

Abdoul-Aziz: Well, it depends on the situation. I speak English at work and school. But I speak French with my friends. And I speak Hausa, an African language, when I call my family back home.

Interviewer: Isn't it hard for you to keep switching languages?

Abdoul-Aziz: Yes, it feels very strange, like changing my identity every time I switch in and out of English. I keep asking myself: Who am I? Am I African? Am I American? Or am I a mixture of both?

Interviewer: And does that feeling ever get any easier?

Abdoul-Aziz: Yes, because as my English gets better, I find that I'm changing. I think I'm becoming more and more American these days. My mother says I'm not as formal as I used to be.

Narrator: Now complete the steps in your book.

Narrator: **Chapter 4, Diversity in Today's United States**
Page 59
Note taking: Listening for definitions, Step 2

Narrator: One.

Betty Jordon: A metaphor is an image, a picture, or a model that is used to help us understand things that are very complex, like societies.

Narrator: Two.

Betty Jordon: A melting pot is a large metal pot – a kind of container – that's used for melting things, such as different foods.

Narrator: Three.

Betty Jordon: A salad is a dish made of different vegetables that are mixed together.

Narrator: Four.

Betty Jordon: A patchwork quilt is a cover for a bed and it's made from pieces of colorful cloth sewn together.

Narrator: Five.

Betty Jordon: A kaleidoscope is a toy that you look through, and if you turn it, you can see beautiful, changing patterns.

Narrator: Now complete the steps in your book.

**Narrator: Chapter 4, Diversity in Today's United States
Page 60
Note taking: Using numbers to organize your notes, Step 2**

Betty Jordon: American society is more diverse and more complex than ever. Over the years historians and writers have used different metaphors to try to describe this complex American culture, and what I'd like to do today is first to describe four of those metaphors to you. Then, in the second part of the lecture I'll talk about transnationalism, a word that describes the relationship that recent immigrants continue to have with their home countries.

All right. To begin, let's talk about what a metaphor is. So you know a metaphor is an image, a picture, or a model that is used to help us understand things that are very complex, like societies. It's a kind of comparison.

Let's look at our first slide here. This is probably the oldest metaphor for describing American society. It's a melting pot. A melting pot is a large metal pot – a kind of container – that's used for melting things, such as different foods. You put different ingredients in the pot, heat it, and the ingredients all melt together and become something new. The picture you're looking at is of a fondue – that's a dish from Switzerland that has cheese and other ingredients – but it's melted so the original ingredients disappear, and the result is something new and different. This metaphor became popular at the beginning of the twentieth century. And so according to this metaphor, all immigrants coming into the U.S. would lose their separate identities and assimilate, or mix with the people who were already here, and everybody would come together to create a new and unique culture. You see?

But one problem with this metaphor is that it doesn't always describe reality, especially today's reality, which is that although some immigrants do assimilate, many of them have a different experience. For example, some groups are not accepted by the larger society, or maybe they don't want to mix in completely. So instead, what happens is that many immigrants keep parts of their own cultural identity. For example, they may continue to speak their own language. They may celebrate their own traditional holidays. They usually marry someone from their own race – their own ethnic group. And they might never say they are American, even if they live here most of their lives.

So, if the melting pot isn't a good metaphor for describing American culture, what is? Let's look at the next slide here: a salad in a salad bowl. Of course, a salad is a dish made of different vegetables that are mixed together, but in a salad, each ingredient keeps its own color and taste. So this metaphor represents America as a diverse culture made of different races, ethnic groups, cultures, and languages that live together, but each group may keep parts of its own culture.

Some people prefer other metaphors for America, like the patchwork quilt. A patchwork quilt is a cover for a bed and it's made from pieces of colorful cloth sewn together. Some people like this picture of America because it shows that we're all unique but we're all connected, like the pieces of a quilt. And then a fourth metaphor – you see it here – is a kaleidoscope. A kaleidoscope is a toy that you look through, and if you turn it, you can see beautiful, changing patterns. This is the metaphor I like best because it's very dynamic. What I mean is that it shows America as a beautiful picture – a multiracial, multiethnic, multicultural society that is always changing.

Narrator: Now complete the steps in your book.

Narrator: Chapter 4, Diversity in Today's United States
Page 63
Note taking: Using bullets to organize your notes, Step 2

Betty Jordon: So, today's immigrants often keep parts of their own cultural identity at the same time as they become part of mainstream American society.

Today's immigrants also maintain some kind of relationship with their countries of origin – I mean the countries where they or their parents were born. And the word that's used to describe this relationship is *transnationalism*, which comes from *trans*, meaning across, and nationalism, which is of course related to the word *nation*; so a transnational is a person whose experience goes across nations or cultures.

Let me give you some examples of that. Many immigrants own homes, land, or businesses in their country of origin. For instance, I have a student who's building a vacation home in the Dominican Republic even though he lives in New York. Other examples . . . immigrants may send money to family members in their native countries. They might continue to support sports teams there. They may travel home frequently and they may even get involved in business or political affairs there. My neighbor, who's Korean, has a business in Seoul in addition to his business in the U.S. He travels there at least five or six times a year to take care of it.

Now, why do you think immigrants today have a closer relationship with their home countries than immigrants did in the past? Well, there are different

factors that make this possible, like ease of travel and technology. See, air travel is now more convenient and less expensive than it was 40 or 50 years ago, so people can go back and forth between the U.S. and their homeland more often. Second, communication technology has advanced, too, so it's easy for people to stay in contact by phone or by Internet. It's also easier to send money to other countries.

So I hope our discussion has helped you to see that immigrants today have a complex relationship with their new country, America, as well as their countries of origin.

Narrator: Now complete the steps in your book.

5

Narrator: CD 2
Chapter 5, The Struggle Begins
Page 67
Building background knowledge, Step 2

Narrator: One.
Man: This is a picture of the Declaration of Independence, adopted on July 4, 1776.

Narrator: Two.
Woman: This is a photograph of the leaders of the Seneca Falls Convention, held in 1848.

Narrator: Three.
Man: This painting shows people celebrating the end of slavery in 1865.

Narrator: Four.
Woman: This photo shows an African-American man drinking water at a segregated water fountain. It was taken during the Jim Crow era, which lasted from about 1880 until the 1960s.

Narrator: Five.
Man: This picture shows American women demonstrating for the right to vote. Women won this right in 1920, when the U.S. Congress passed the Nineteenth Amendment.

Narrator: Six.

Woman: This photo shows African Americans protesting school segregation. Legal segregation of public schools ended in 1954 in a case called *Brown versus Board of Education of Topeka*.

Narrator: Now complete the steps in your book.

**Narrator: Chapter 5, The Struggle Begins
Page 71
Listening for answers to *Wh-* questions,
Step 2**

Interviewer: Hi, Cynthia, can you tell me a little bit about yourself?

Cynthia: Well, I'm from New York, but my family's from the South. My parents were raised in South Carolina.

Interviewer: Well, what I'd like to ask you about today is your childhood in the early 1950s because I'm wondering what it was like before the civil rights movement.

Cynthia: I was a young girl then . . .

Interviewer: And what do you remember from that period?

Cynthia: Well, one very clear memory I have is that in August every year, my parents would take us down on a long trip from New York to the South to reconnect with the family down there.

Interviewer: How did you get down there?

Cynthia: Well, we traveled by car. So we'd fill the car with pillows for all the children, and we took all kinds of things to eat because we weren't sure you could buy food on the road. You had to plan the food you might need – snacks for the children, sandwiches . . .

Interviewer: Were you aware of segregation in the South?

Cynthia: Well, I'm going to tell you about the moment when I think I really became aware. On one of these trips, I remember that we stopped at a gas station, and I jumped out of the car, and ran over to get a drink of water from the water fountain. And before I knew it, the owner of the gas station came over and grabbed me. And he

swung me around, and pointed to the sign that said "Whites only." And he shouted, "Can't you read?"

Interviewer: Really! What was your reaction?

Cynthia: Well, I was really startled.

Interviewer: And then what happened?

Cynthia: Well, my father came over, and he seemed really angry, and he made me get back in the car. I ran over and jumped into the back seat, and we drove off. And I kept asking my father why he was so angry. But he wouldn't speak for a long, long time. And then finally, many miles down the road, he stopped the car and he told us to never, ever leave my mother or him. Because he couldn't guarantee our safety. And I remember really being upset. No one said anything.

Interviewer: Oh, I can imagine what a terrible experience that was for all of you.

Cynthia: Yes, it was. And you know, in recent years, I've tried to talk to my family about that event. My father still doesn't want to talk about it. About how helpless he felt, not being able to protect his family. My mother talks about how hard it was for him to be in that position, to not be able to protect his daughter.

Interviewer: That period had a dramatic impact on so many people.

Cynthia: Yes. And although we see progress, and are positive and optimistic about the changes that have occurred, there are still challenges.

Interviewer: Thank you very much, Cynthia.

Cynthia: You're welcome.

Narrator: Now complete the steps in your book.

**Narrator: Chapter 5, The Struggle Begins
Page 72
Listening for specific information,
Step 2**

Interviewer: Hilda, can you talk a little bit about the changes you've seen for women since you were younger?

Hilda: Well, you know, since I was born, incredible changes have come about.

Interviewer: Do you mind if I ask how old you are now?

Hilda: No, not at all. I'm in my 60s. And when I went to high school back in the '50s, the typical family was really different from what you see today. Back then, everyone had a specific role.

Interviewer: What do you mean?

Hilda: Well, there was a father who worked outside the house, a mother who was a housewife, and usually two or three children.

Interviewer: Did your family fit that description?

Hilda: Yes, my mother stayed home and took care of the children, and in fact all the women I knew did, too. My brother went to college – he was the first one in the family, actually – but there was never any discussion of *me* going to college. Women didn't go to college. They got married and then they had children. You know what people used to say, "You don't need a college education to change diapers."

Interviewer: So in other words, they expected you to settle down and get married.

Hilda: Yes. But I had a dream. I said that when I grew up, I wanted to be a secretary. I know that doesn't sound very exciting today, but back then, that was my dream. So I studied typing in high school, and then I graduated and worked as a secretary. I felt as if I was really making progress. Actually, it took awhile until I realized that I could do even better than that.

Interviewer: And what happened to make you realize that?

Hilda: Well, in 1965 there was a big women's demonstration in Chicago, where I lived. And I went, and it was phenomenal. The streets were full of women protesting. They wanted to have the same opportunities as men did – to be able to work in any job they wanted to. And you know, those kinds of demands opened my eyes. I thought, I can get an education and make something of myself. So after that, I walked into college and registered.

Interviewer: You did?! Good for you!

Hilda: Yes, and I went to college, and my whole life changed. I became a teacher. Maybe that doesn't seem so exciting either, but back then, that was a big deal. Today, the situation is so much better. Young girls can be anything they like. You know, you look around and there are women everywhere. The bus driver can be a woman, or the doctor can be a woman, or the teacher can be a man! That's what I mean when I say things have changed incredibly.

Narrator: Now complete the steps in your book.

**Narrator: Chapter 5, The Struggle Begins Page 75
Note taking: Listening for guiding questions, Step 2**

Narrator: One.

Julia Smith: So these are just a few examples of important events in the early struggle for civil rights. What happened next? Well, these events led to more protests, more demonstrations, and more sit-ins throughout the '60s.

Narrator: Two.

Julia Smith: Today we can look back and be thankful for the great achievements of the civil rights movement. What were some of these achievements? Well first, the Jim Crow laws were overturned.

Narrator: Three.

Julia Smith: A journalist named Betty Friedan wrote a book called *The Feminine Mystique*. It was based on interviews with white, middle-class women living in the suburbs, and what do you think Friedan discovered? That these women were very unhappy with their lives, with their lack of freedom and lack of a sense of identity.

Narrator: Four.

Julia Smith: Was the women's movement successful? In some ways yes, of course. Today "equal pay for equal work" is the law.

Narrator: Now complete the steps in your book.

Narrator: Chapter 5, The Struggle Begins
Page 77
Note taking: Creating your own symbols and abbreviations, Step 3

Julia Smith: So to begin, the '60s was a time of great and often violent change in the United States. There were many political and social movements. Two important ones were the civil rights movement and the women's movement. They involved thousands of people all over the nation and led to new laws that gave us many of the rights we have today.

First I'm going to talk about the civil rights movement – the struggle by hundreds of thousands of people working over many years to achieve equal rights for African Americans. And it started because, almost 100 years after the end of slavery in the United States, segregation and discrimination against blacks was still common. For example, blacks in many states still couldn't eat in the same places as whites, or swim in the same swimming pools, or sit down on a bus if a white person was standing. The anger that black people felt, and many white people, too, over these unfair conditions is what started the civil rights movement.

It's difficult to point to the year that the movement began, but there were several key historical events. On December 1, 1955, in the city of Montgomery, in Alabama, a black woman named Rosa Parks refused to give up her bus seat to a white person. This led to the famous Montgomery bus boycott. For one year the entire black community refused to ride on the city buses. The bus company lost a great deal of money and, in the end, the Alabama courts ruled that racial segregation on buses was unconstitutional, and the city of Montgomery was forced to change its policy.

A few years later, in 1960, black students in North Carolina refused to leave a restaurant when the owner wouldn't serve them food because of their color.

This kind of protest – they were called sit-ins because people would sit and refuse to leave – this kind of protest soon spread like fire all over the South. And how many of you have heard of Martin Luther King, Jr.? Well, in 1963, there was a huge national demonstration in Washington, D.C., called the March on Washington, where about 200,000 people heard King give his famous speech: "I Have a Dream."

So these are just a few examples of important events in the early struggle for civil rights. What happened next? Well, these events led to more protests, more demonstrations, and more sit-ins throughout the '60s, with hundreds of thousands of ordinary people, black and white, struggling together to stop prejudice and discrimination.

Today we can look back and be thankful for the great achievements of the civil rights movement. What were some of these achievements? Well first, the Jim Crow laws were overturned. This meant that segregation became illegal. Second, the federal government passed laws, like the Civil Rights Act of 1964 and the Voting Rights Act of 1965, which guaranteed the rights of black Americans. Finally, and maybe most important of all, the successes of the civil rights movement led other groups to begin fighting for justice and equality.

Narrator: Now complete the steps in your book.

Narrator: Chapter 5, The Struggle Begins
Page 79
Note taking: Organizing your notes in a chart, Step 2

Julia Smith: Now, the women's rights movement was related in some ways to the civil rights movement, and that's what we'll turn to next. I'm going to tell you about some important events in the history of the movement from the 1940s until today and talk about the movement's main achievements.

Now, were you aware that during World War II, when thousands of men were fighting in Europe and Asia, women took over the men's jobs? They worked in factories, in construction, in offices, anywhere they were needed. However, in 1945, when the men returned from the war, the women had to leave those jobs and go back home, back to their roles as wives and mothers. But by the 1950s, more and more women were feeling dissatisfied with these roles.

You see, although about 30 percent of women worked, they were often paid much less, less than half of what men earned, even if they were doing the same job. Plus, women didn't have the same opportunities as men. They could be teachers or nurses or secretaries. The few women working in business had almost no chance to become managers or executives, even if they were qualified and worked hard.

Then, in 1963, a journalist named Betty Friedan wrote a book called *The Feminine Mystique*. It was based on interviews with white, middle-class women living in the suburbs, and what do you think Friedan discovered? That these women were very unhappy with their lives, with their lack of freedom and lack of a sense of identity. This book shocked America. It became a huge best seller, and nowadays, looking back, we can say it marked the beginning of the modern women's movement.

Starting in the mid-1960s, after *The Feminine Mystique* came out, women began to organize and work hard for equal opportunity. They marched in the streets, they tried to elect more women to Congress, they gave speeches, they wrote letters. They demanded equal opportunities for women in education and at work. They asked, "Why shouldn't women be able to be doctors, lawyers, business professionals, as well as police officers, firefighters, construction workers?" Professions that traditionally women couldn't do, you see.

And another one of their key demands was "equal pay for equal work."

So looking back, was the women's movement successful? In some ways, yes, of course. Today "equal pay for equal work" is the law. More women than men go to college these days. More students in medical school are women than men. There are women politicians and university presidents. It is certainly true that women today have more control over their lives than they did 50 years ago. But we still have work to do. For example, women today still earn only about 87 cents for every dollar that a man earns, and if a woman has a baby, she usually has to return to work in 12 weeks or lose her job. So we've made great progress, but inequalities still exist.

Narrator: Now complete the steps in your book.

6

Narrator: Chapter 6, The Struggle Continues
Page 82
Listening for specific information,
Step 2

Narrator: One.

Peter: My name is Peter. I'm 55 years old, and five months ago I lost my job as a computer programmer after working for the same company for 16 years. My boss said the company was losing money and didn't have enough work for me to do. But I heard that they just hired a new programmer who's 26 years old.

Narrator: Two.

Theresa: My name is Theresa, and I'm a journalist. Last week I had a job interview at a magazine. The interview went great until the end, when suddenly the interviewer asked me if I was pregnant. I told him the truth – yes, I am pregnant, but I plan to continue working after my baby is born. But, well, I didn't get the job.

Narrator: Three.

Robert: My name is Robert. I'm married and I have three children. Last week my wife and I filled out an application to rent a new apartment. It's close to my work, and a good friend of ours also lives in the building. Our friend told the manager that we are quiet, responsible people, but we didn't get the apartment. Our friend thinks it's because nobody else in the building has children and the manager is worried that our kids will make noise.

Narrator: Four.

Rebecca: My name is Rebecca. I'm a university student and I use a wheelchair. One of my classes is on the eighth floor and the building has only two elevators, so I've been late to class a few times. I explained the problem to the professor, but he says it doesn't matter. He expects me to get to class on time – just like everybody else.

Narrator: Now complete the steps in your book.

Narrator: Chapter 6, The Struggle Continues
Page 84
Listening for specific information,
Step 2

Interviewer: Hi, Robin. I understand you work with the blind.

Robin: Yes, that's right. I work with people who are either partly or completely blind, and basically, I try to help them participate fully and equally in our society, especially at work.

Interviewer: At work?

Robin: Sure, because for example there are lots of office jobs that blind people can do nowadays, now that there are computers that can talk, and software that prints documents in Braille.

Interviewer: Really?

Robin: And work is really important for people. It gives them something to do. It gives them a reason to get out of bed in the morning – an identity, you know, something

to talk about – and of course, it also gives them a salary.

Interviewer: So what exactly do you do?

Robin: Well, I help them learn the basic skills they need to become independent.

Interviewer: Could you give me some examples?

Robin: If you think about your day, just the little things that are involved in getting up and getting out of the door and getting to work – try to imagine doing all that without being able to see. But there are many simple gadgets and techniques that can help blind people function better.

Interviewer: Like what?

Robin: Well, for example, it's useful to have a talking clock. It's just like a regular clock, but it says the time. And there are other items, too, that make life easier, like a tray, which is one of the simplest aids that blind people can use.

Interviewer: A tray? How would they use a tray?

Robin: A tray helps you to keep all your things together. If you put something down on the tray, you know exactly where it is, so you can pick it up again.

Interviewer: Ah, interesting.

Robin: Yes. And then there's money. By folding a bill a certain way, you can tell what kind of bill it is. You leave singles flat. You fold fives from side to side, and tens from top to bottom. You fold twenties both ways.

Interviewer: I would never have thought of that.

Robin: Well, you see, these are simple things that help blind people to live regular lives. Imagine people feeling that their problems are overwhelming, and then they learn how to do things on their own, and it's as if a new world has opened to them. That's why I love my job.

Interviewer: Thank you, Robin, very much.

Narrator: Now complete the steps in your book.

Narrator: Chapter 6, The Struggle Continues
Page 85
Listening for main ideas, Step 2

Interviewer: Hello, Jairo. You're Latino, right?

Jairo: Yeah. I was born in Colombia, but I moved to the United States many years ago.

Interviewer: And you're a teacher.

Jairo: Yes. I teach history.

Interviewer: Well then, let me ask you this question: Do you think Latinos have made progress over the past 50 years or so?

Jairo: Well, I would say that as a group, Latinos have made important contributions to American society – because we're the largest minority group in the United States – so there are Latinos at every level of American life, I mean sports, entertainment, education . . . everywhere. And we've made important political progress, too. About 300 cities have mayors who are Latinos, and there are more Latino members in Congress.

Interviewer: How about some other examples of progress?

Jairo: Well, for example, politicians and also businesses recognize that there is a need to provide services and products in Spanish. So, for example, now in hospitals, when patients come in, there are interpreters, so the patients don't have to struggle to explain their symptoms in English.

Interviewer: That's great!

Jairo: And by the way, that is also true for people who speak other languages, like Russian or Korean. There's more help for people who don't speak English than there was before.

Interviewer: And what about the future? What other progress would you like to see?

Jairo: Well, there's still a lot of poverty in the Hispanic community. Over 20 percent of Latinos still live below the poverty level, compared to only 10 percent for the rest of the population. And poverty creates other problems, of course. Large numbers of Latinos can't get good health care or high quality education. I hope that will improve in the future.

Interviewer: I hope you're right, Jairo. Thanks. Now, what about you, Sandy? Is there another group that's made progress toward equality, in your opinion?

Sandy: Well, I think that there has been some progress for senior citizens. I mean, since the 1960s it's been illegal to discriminate against people because of their age.

Interviewer: Could you give me an example?

Sandy: Well, at work, for example, it's illegal to hire or fire someone because of their age.

Interviewer: And does that mean it never happens anymore?

Sandy: Unfortunately, no. Let me tell you about my father. See, he's in his late 50s now, and recently he lost his job when his company was sold. And you know, he's had a lot of trouble finding a new one. And I'm sure it's because of his age.

Interviewer: But didn't you just say there was a law protecting the rights of older workers?

Sandy: Well, yes, there are laws, but they're really hard to enforce. A lot of times the boss thinks there's a risk to hiring older people. They might get sick, and of course they also get higher salaries because they have more experience. But the boss won't say this, so there's no obvious discrimination, but he'll think it. And if he's got two applicants for a job, and one is older and the other one is younger, he'll hire the younger one. That's what happened to my dad.

Interviewer: So what you're saying is that we still need to work towards changing people's stereotypes about older people.

Sandy: Definitely.

Narrator: Now complete the steps in your book.

Narrator: Chapter 6, The Struggle Continues
Page 91
Note taking: Listening for signal words and phrases, Step 2

Narrator: One.

David Chachere: Now to refresh your memory, the '60s was an important decade because during this time, several important laws gave more rights to women, African Americans, and immigrants.

Narrator: Two.

David Chachere: Let's begin with the first one, the Age Discrimination Act. I think we need to talk about first, the reasons why this law was needed; second, what it does; and third, its impact.

Narrator: Three.

David Chachere: Before this law, employers could set an age limit for job applicants.

Narrator: Four.

David Chachere: Well, of course, it refers to hiring and firing. In other words, age can't be used as a reason for refusing to hire an older person.

Narrator: Five.

David Chachere: In addition, age can't be used as a reason to promote someone to a better position.

Narrator: Six.

David Chachere: The ADA also covers people who face discrimination because they have a serious illness like cancer.

Narrator: Seven.

David Chachere: And as for nonphysical disabilities, did you know that some businesses are actually starting to hire some people with mental disabilities if they are capable of doing a particular job?

Narrator: Eight.

David Chachere: But I think the most important impact of this law is that it's helped to change the way we think.

Narrator: Nine.

David Chachere: In many places in the world, people with disabilities have to stay at home because there is no way for them to get around.

Narrator: Now complete the steps in your book.

**Narrator: Chapter 6, The Struggle Continues
Page 93
Note taking: Indenting, Step 2**

David Chachere: Hello, everyone. Now to refresh your memory, the '60s was an important decade because during this time, several important laws gave more rights to women, African Americans, and immigrants. But today I'll talk about two other groups: the elderly – I mean senior citizens – and the disabled. The laws that I'll talk about specifically are the Age Discrimination in Employment Act of 1967 and the Americans with Disabilities Act of 1990.

Let's begin with the first one, the Age Discrimination Act. I think we need to talk about first, the reasons why this law was needed; second, what it does; and third, its impact.

So first of all, why did the United States need this law? Well, the law tried to correct several problems, mainly, that older people faced a lot of discrimination in the workplace. Before this law, employers could set an age limit for job applicants. For example, they might say that a job was open only to applicants under age 35.

The law tries to change this situation. Basically, it protects people over 40 years old from discrimination at work and it covers a lot of areas. Well, of course, it refers to hiring and firing. In other words, age can't be used as a reason for refusing to hire an older person, and employers cannot fire older people because of their age, either. In addition, age can't be used as a reason to promote someone to a better position or give them particular jobs.

The impact of this law has been quite significant. If you're applying for a job nowadays, you won't see anything about age on the application. And a second example is that older workers can get the same benefits as younger people – health insurance, and so on. Also, in most cases, mandatory retirement is not allowed nowadays. In other words, your company cannot force you to retire.

You might ask: Do employers actually follow this law? Well, there are still many thousands of legal complaints about age discrimination each year, so we have to be realistic about this. There is still some discrimination against older workers. For example, a recent study showed that companies are more than 40 percent more likely to interview a younger job applicant than an older job applicant. However, people are definitely more aware of age discrimination than they were before.

Narrator: Now complete the steps in your book.

Narrator: Chapter 6, The Struggle Continues
Page 94
Note taking: Using an outline, Step 3

David Chachere: Now let's turn to the second law – the Americans with Disabilities Act, which is often called the ADA for short. This law was passed in 1990 and it protects people with disabilities against discrimination in different places, for example, at work, in housing, and in education.

By "disability" we mean first, any physical or mental condition that limits a person's ability to participate in a major life activity like walking, seeing, or hearing. The ADA also covers people who face discrimination because they have a serious illness like cancer – so both physical and mental disabilities.

Let me describe the impact of the ADA. This law has changed life for thousands of disabled people across the country. If you've ridden a public bus in an American city, for example, you know that they all have special mechanisms to help people in wheelchairs get on and off the bus. And doorways have to be wide for the same reason – so that people in wheelchairs can easily get in and out of buildings. And as for non-physical disabilities, did you know that some businesses are actually starting to hire some people with mental disabilities if they are capable of doing a particular

job? And students with learning difficulties can get help, such as extra time on tests.

But I think the most important impact of this law is that it's helped to change the way we think. In many places in the world, people with disabilities have to stay at home because there is no way for them to get around, and they are also often rejected by society. We are beginning to understand that having a disability doesn't mean people can't participate in society, and there are many things people with particular disabilities can do. In 1990, when President George H. W. Bush signed the Americans with Disabilities Act into law, he said, "Let the shameful wall of exclusion finally come tumbling down." In other words, that the wall that had always separated disabled people from everyone else should disappear. What this means is that our goal needs to be inclusion – equality and full participation for all people, including people with disabilities.

Narrator: Now complete the steps in your book.

7

Narrator: Chapter 7, American Values from the Past
Page 99
Listening for specific information, Step 2

Man: Ben's parents have died. Even though he has few friends, he refuses to lose hope. His motto is: wait and hope. His positive spirit impresses a rich stranger, who gives him a job. Ben is also a very good student who wins an academic competition at school. Because of his good luck and determination, Ben is eventually accepted to Harvard University.

Narrator: Now complete the steps in your book.

Narrator: Chapter 7, American Values from the Past
Page 102
Answering true/false/not sure questions, Step 2

Interviewer: Marielena, what values do you think are particularly important? For example, what values do you try to teach your daughter?

Marielena: Let's see. I've been thinking a lot about that lately. I'm trying to teach her the importance of independence. I want her to be able to take control of her life.

Interviewer: Your daughter's only 12, isn't she? Isn't that a little early to think about being independent?

Marielena: No, I don't think so. See, I want her to realize that she has a lot of options. There's a lot of pressure in school to do well, and the expectation in my family is that the children will become professionals, you know, lawyers or architects, that sort of thing.

Interviewer: Don't you agree with that?

Marielena: Not really. I think people should have choices, and I think there are many ways to be happy and productive. I want her to find a career that's suitable and meaningful for her, something that will make her happy. I think maybe she'll become an artist – a painter, a singer, an actress, or a chef! What's important is that she make her own decisions.

Interviewer: What if she's not happy being an artist or a chef?

Marielena: Well, she can do something else. You can change professions, you know, no matter how old you are. I have a friend who's in his late 30s and works in a hospital, but he just went back to college because he wants to study to be a lawyer. Nobody told him he shouldn't do it, even though he's one of the oldest students in the class.

Interviewer: That's great! Well now, Dan, what do you think are some important values?

Dan: Well, the first thing I think of is hard work. And self-reliance. These values are repeated everywhere you look. For example, politicians are always talking about the value of hard work and personal responsibility.

Interviewer: Is personal responsibility the same as self-reliance?

Dan: Yeah, you know, depending on yourself and trying to improve yourself. Not expecting other people to take care of you.

Interviewer: I know you've just started college. Do you study hard?

Dan: Yes. Because I know that if I want to do well, I have to study hard. I put a lot of effort into my studies. I also just started working part-time at a bookstore, and I really like working.

Interviewer: Oh, really?

Dan: Yeah, I think that working helps you to prepare for life after college. It's important to work toward goals that you set for yourself. And I also see work as being my duty and my obligation because I don't want to keep asking my family for money. Since I got a job, I have my own spending money and I can do whatever I like with it.

Narrator: Now complete the steps in your book.

Narrator: Chapter 7, American Values from the Past
Page 103
Listening for main ideas, Step 2

Interviewer: Hi, Anne-Marie and Leila. We've just been discussing values, and I want to ask you if you can give me an example of a typical American value that you don't agree with. Anne-Marie? Do you have one?

Anne-Marie: Yeah, informality. Most Americans are very informal – in fact I think perhaps we're too informal.

Interviewer: How do you mean?

Anne-Marie: Well, you know, I went to the opera the other day, and I saw people wearing jeans. I think that's unbelievable. Americans wear jeans everywhere they go.

Interviewer: What's wrong with that?

Anne-Marie: Well, I think people should wear something more formal if they're going to the opera or a nice restaurant. It's a matter of respect. Of course you want to be comfortable, but I do think there's a limit.

Interviewer: Can you think of another example of informality?

Anne-Marie: Yeah. People treat each other on a first-name basis these days, for example, in banks and doctors' offices. Now that is way too informal. It makes me feel uncomfortable to have the bank teller call me Anne-Marie, as if I were a kid. I'm an adult, and I think it's disrespectful. These days even college professors tell students to call them by their first names. I'm not comfortable with that, either.

Interviewer: And Leila, what's your opinion? Can you give me a typical value that you disagree with?

Leila: Well, I was going to talk about directness. I think it's good to be honest, but sometimes I think we Americans are too direct.

Interviewer: For example?

Leila: Well, in a discussion, for instance. People say things like, "You're totally wrong," or "I don't agree with you at all." It's not like that in other countries I've visited. People are more tactful.

Interviewer: So you think we're too direct?

Leila: Yes! Here's another example. I learned about this when I was traveling in Europe and Asia. Let's say you're eating in someone's house, and they ask you if you'd like some more. You're supposed to say, "No, thanks."

Interviewer: Even if you'd like some more food?

Leila: Yes, because you don't want to be greedy. So you say, "No, thanks," and then your host insists and finally you say, "Oh, well, maybe just a little bit more." We're not like that in America. We just accept, right away.

Interviewer: But what's wrong with that?

Leila: Well, I think we're too direct. It's rude. I have another good example. Listen to this. Once we had a new neighbor, and she came over, and the first thing she said was, "Aren't you going to show me around?" It was as if she expected it. And then she wanted to use the phone, but she didn't ask, "Could I use the phone?" Instead, she said, "Where's the phone?" And here's another example. I took an American friend of mine to my mother's house, and he went straight for the refrigerator and helped himself to some juice. He didn't even ask!

Interviewer: What did your mother say?

Leila: She was a little surprised, I think.

Narrator: Now complete the steps in your book.

Narrator: Chapter 7, American Values from the Past
Page 107
Note taking: Listening for key words, Step 1

Narrator: One.

Peter Roman: This afternoon I'm going to talk about three traditional American folk heroes. And by folk heroes I mean real people or imaginary figures who do extraordinary things, or who have extraordinary powers.

Narrator: Two.

Peter Roman: Let's begin with the cowboy. Think about all the places you see cowboys. If you turn on the TV, I guarantee you'll find a cowboy movie on one of the channels! And the image of the cowboy is also seen constantly in advertising and fashion.

Narrator: Three.

Peter Roman: An entrepreneur is a person who starts a company – who makes business deals in order to make a profit. We think of entrepreneurs as people who have great ideas and take risks. And the entrepreneur is also a very powerful symbol of American values.

Narrator: Four.

Peter Roman: There are all kinds of superheroes – Superman, Batman, Spider-Man, and so on. And superheroes – well, if you can't save yourself, they will!

Narrator: Now complete the steps in your book.

Narrator: Chapter 7, American Values from the Past
Page 108
Note taking: Clarifying your notes, Step 2

Peter Roman: Hello, everyone. This afternoon I'm going to talk about three traditional American folk heroes. And by folk heroes I mean real people or imaginary figures who do extraordinary things, or who have extraordinary powers. The United States, like every country, has many of these traditional folk heroes, but I want to talk about three famous ones, and they are the cowboy, the entrepreneur, and the superhero. In this country, we see these three images everywhere – in the media, in advertising. . . . They represent some of our most important values, and I think that's why they're so popular.

So, let's begin with the cowboy. Think about all the places you see cowboys. If you turn on the TV, I guarantee you'll find a cowboy movie on one of the channels! And the image of the cowboy is also seen constantly in advertising and fashion. In fact, I bet that 90 percent of the people in this room are probably wearing jeans!

Why do you think the cowboy is such a popular image in our culture? Well, let's go back in history about 150 years. During the nineteenth century, people began moving west in order to make their fortune. Some of these settlers started large cattle ranches and hired cowboys. Over time the cowboy became a classic American hero. Think about it: The cowboy works alone, in difficult weather and dangerous conditions. He is completely self-reliant. He never seems to need money or anything like that! He represents courage, freedom, and independence – qualities that almost all Americans still value today.

OK, so next, let's go on to talk about the entrepreneur. An entrepreneur is a person who starts a company – who makes business deals in order to make a profit. We think of entrepreneurs as people who have great ideas and take risks. And the entrepreneur is also a very powerful symbol of American values. That's because entrepreneurs represent the idea that if you're smart, if you work hard, and if you have good ideas, you can succeed. This kind of success story has been popular ever since the Horatio Alger stories of the early twentieth century. And although many young Americans have never heard of Horatio Alger, they certainly know Bill Gates or other successful people who have become American heroes because of their talent, their belief in themselves, and the risks that they take.

Now, the last American hero I'd like you to think about is imaginary. This is the superhero, who we find in comic books, movies, and television. There are all kinds of superheroes – Superman, Batman, Spider-Man, and so on. And superheroes – well, if you can't save yourself, they will! They're fast and they're powerful. They're symbols of justice and law. That's why Superman is always defending the good guys and punishing the bad guys. Most Americans relate very strongly to the values that the superhero represents, and that's why this image is so popular in our culture.

Narrator: Now complete the steps in your book.

Narrator: Chapter 7, American Values from the Past
Page 110
Note taking: Taking notes on questions and answers, Step 2

Peter Roman: All right, are there any questions?
Student: Professor Roman, could you explain a little more about entrepreneurs? Are they always very successful?
Peter Roman: Well, some of them aren't successful; others are. But after the Civil War, there was a period of huge industrial expansion in the United States. Thousands of miles of railroads were built and that made it possible for industries like steel and oil to grow. And since that time there

have been some entrepreneurs who have been very, very successful and become extremely rich. Have you ever heard of, let's see, Andrew Carnegie? He made millions of dollars from his steel factories. Oh, and I bet you've heard of John D. Rockefeller. He made his fortune in oil. Carnegie and Rockefeller were two of our earliest entrepreneur-heroes. Another question?

Student: Did Superman also exist in the nineteenth century?

Peter Roman: No, the first Superman comic book was written a little later, in the 1930s, and the other superhero characters came after that. Have you seen the movie *The Incredibles*? It was about a whole family of characters with superpowers. It was one of the most profitable movies in history! If I remember correctly, it made more than $500 million dollars. It seems like Americans never get tired of the superhero image.

Student: Professor, I have a question. Why didn't you talk about any women folk heroes?

Peter Roman: Yes, I thought about that. The thing is, there are very few traditional folk heroes who are women. There was a woman named Annie Oakley in the nineteenth century who was famous for her shooting skills. At a time when most women were wives and mothers, she traveled around and had shooting competitions with men. Also, she gave a lot of the money she made to different charities. And then there's Wonder Woman, the comic book superhero. She first appeared in 1941. But most of the traditional folk heroes have been men, although I'm sure that's going to change in the future.

Narrator: Now complete the steps in your book.

Narrator: CD 3
Chapter 8, American Values Today
Page 114
Listening for specific information, Step 2

Woman: I've just been reading this article about Generation Y. That's you, isn't it?

Man: Yeah, I think so. I was born in 1985. So what does the article say about me?

Woman: Well, it says there are between 70 and 76 million Generation Y-ers in America.

Man: Is that a lot?

Woman: Sure. It's about 20 percent of the population! Generation Y is as big as the Baby Boom generation and about six times as big as Generation X, which is the generation that came right before.

Man: What else does the article say?

Woman: It talks about the values of your generation.

Man: Like what?

Woman: Well, for example, it says you have a tolerance for diversity. It says Generation Y-ers are very open and tolerant. And then . . . now this is interesting, speed and constant change – you're the Internet generation so you don't like to wait for things.

Man: That's true. What else?

Woman: It says you value independence, money, and social responsibility! Is that true?

Man: Yeah, I think we do. I think we should do what we can to make the world a better place.

Narrator: Now complete the steps in your book.

Narrator: Chapter 8, American Values Today
Page 116
Drawing inferences, Step 1

Interviewer: Rosiane, do you think that your own values are very different from the values of your parents?

Rosiane: Oh, yeah, I think they are different. My parents have very traditional values.

Like they wanted me to meet a nice guy, get married when I was about 20 and have kids, so they could help bring up the grandchildren. But I didn't really want to do that.

Interviewer: What did you want?

Rosiane: Well, I guess I wanted more independence. When I was in my early 20s, I wasn't looking for a husband – I was busy looking for a career. I studied hard, and then I became an accountant. It took me a long time to reach that point. I'm 33 now and just recently got married, so I don't have any kids yet.

Interviewer: What do your parents think about your choices?

Rosiane: Well, even though my values are different from theirs, they accepted my decisions.

Interviewer: Dan-el, how about you?

Dan-el: Well, I think I see eye to eye with my parents on many general values, like . . . the importance of respect. My mother always taught me that I had to respect other people, no matter who they were or what they thought. But I guess my parents and I disagree on a lot of other things, for example, how to raise your children.

Interviewer: What do you disagree about?

Dan-el: Well, let's see . . . I agree with my parents that children need strong discipline. But my parents' generation believes in spanking children. Children get spanked if they stay out late, if they don't do the dishes, if they don't help around the house, and all that . . . but I don't believe in spanking kids. I do believe in discipline, but I don't believe in physical punishment.

Interviewer: I see. Christine, are your values different from your parents' values?

Christine: Well, I'd say my parents are more conservative than I am. I mean, they don't really believe in big changes. My parents and their family – they all live in the same town, and no one has ever moved away. You know, my parents have never even been out of the country.

Interviewer: Never?

Christine: No, in fact, my mom's only been on a plane three times.

Interviewer: And have you been out of the country?

Christine: Well, yeah. I mean, I've already traveled to lots of different places. And I lived in Spain for a while. And I think it's really important to travel because traveling makes you more open-minded.

Interviewer: What do you mean?

Christine: Well, I like having that kind of freedom.

Interviewer: And what about your friends? Do most of them feel the same way?

Christine: Yeah, most of my friends feel the same way. They don't live in the same places as their parents. They move around, because they're exploring and trying to see how they can improve their lives.

Narrator: Now complete the steps in your book.

Narrator: Chapter 8, American Values Today Page 118
Listening for specific information, Step 1

Interviewer: Hi, Sandy. I wanted to interview you because I know you have strong opinions about the values young people need in the workplace.

Sandy: This is true. I'm a business professor and I'm always giving advice to my students about the kind of values they have to develop to succeed. I ask my students, "If you had your own business, would you hire you?"

Interviewer: What values do you think they need?

Sandy: Well, the first thing they need to learn is the value of time. You know what they say: "Time is money." I find that sometimes, students don't respect deadlines. They think, "Well, I don't have to submit my paper on time – it doesn't matter if it's a day or two late," or they arrive for class five minutes after it starts. But they have to learn that that is not acceptable. So I give them an example: Suppose you want to buy a car, and the dealer tells you that the car will be ready Friday at three o'clock in the afternoon. And you go to the dealer, and everything is all paid for – you've paid your deposit and so on. But the dealer tells you, "Well no, I'm sorry, you won't be able to get your car until next Friday." What is your reaction? You're going to be really upset.

Interviewer: Of course, I can see that. What other values are important?

Sandy: Well, the second thing is cooperation and working as a team. And this is very difficult for a lot of our students. They want to be individuals. They want to work alone and show what they can do. They want to stand out. But that is not what we do in the workplace. You don't work in isolation.

Interviewer: But don't you think individual effort is important?

Sandy: Yes, of course it's always important to do your best, but I'd say cooperation is even more important.

Interviewer: And what else?

Sandy: Well, the third value is professionalism. What I mean is, have a professional attitude. You should dress, speak, and write in an appropriate way, according to the situation. See, I believe you should behave professionally at work. And when you speak or write, you should be careful to use a formal tone, especially with customers.

Narrator: Now complete the steps in your book.

Narrator: Chapter 8, American Values Today Page 123
Note taking: Listening for general statements, Step 2

Narrator: One.

Jason Rose: But even though people's values are very diverse, the strongest voices in American politics today do generally fall into two groups – conservative and liberal.

Narrator: Two.

Jason Rose: Conservatives usually put a strong emphasis on personal responsibility.

Narrator: Three.

Jason Rose: Most liberals, on the other hand, think the government should be very active in fixing social problems like poverty and illness.

Narrator: Four.

Jason Rose: Generally, conservatives think government is too big and expensive.

Narrator: Five.

Jason Rose: Conservatives typically believe that the government should stay out of the way of business.

Narrator: Six.

Jason Rose: But in general, liberals believe that government should control and regulate business through strict laws or taxes.

Narrator: Seven.

Jason Rose: The U.S. has two main political parties, so in an election, voters generally choose between the Republicans and the Democrats.

Narrator: Now complete the steps in your book.

Narrator: Chapter 8, American Values Today Page 125
Note taking: Taking notes in a point-by-point format, Step 2

Jason Rose: Good morning, everyone. The focus today will be conservative and liberal values in American politics. Of course, you have to understand that I can only talk about these things in a general way today, because this is a very big topic. It's very hard to make specific statements about Americans' political beliefs since there are more than 300 million Americans from so many different racial, religious, and economic backgrounds. But even though people's values are very diverse, the strongest voices in American politics today do generally fall into two groups – conservative and liberal. So let me outline for you some basic differences between conservatives and liberals in three areas:

the role of the government, taxes, and government regulation of business.

Let's begin with the role of the government. Conservatives usually put a strong emphasis on personal responsibility. They think that people should be responsible for themselves. In other words, they don't believe it's the government's responsibility to pay for social programs that guarantee things like a minimum wage or health insurance. Most liberals, on the other hand, think the government should be very active in fixing social problems like poverty and illness. Liberals believe that it is the responsibility of the government to provide money and help for people who are poor or sick. So for example, they typically support laws that guarantee workers a minimum wage or free lunches at school for poor children.

Now let's move to the second difference I wanted to mention. Generally, conservatives think government is too big and expensive. A big government requires citizens to pay high taxes to support its programs. And, high taxes are not popular with conservatives. But liberals believe taxes are necessary because they help the government provide the services we need for an equal and productive society. Taxes are important because they give the government money to support social programs like the ones I mentioned before. OK?

Finally, conservatives typically believe that the government should stay out of the way of business, that it shouldn't interfere too much in the way business works. They think that an economy without a lot of government control is the best way for the economy to grow and to provide jobs. But in general, liberals believe that government should control and regulate business through strict laws or taxes, because if it doesn't, they think entrepreneurs won't care about their workers or their customers or the environment. They'll only care about

their own profits. So many liberals think business should be closely regulated.

Narrator: Now complete the steps in your book.

Narrator: Chapter 8, American Values Today Page 126
Note taking: Using a handout to help you take notes, Step 2

Jason Rose: Let me remind you that the U.S. has two main political parties, so in an election, voters generally choose between the Republicans and the Democrats. And, in general I think most people associate the Republican Party with conservative values and ideas, and the Democratic Party with liberal ones. But people's values can change over time, and we can see this clearly if we look at the results of the presidential elections of 1964, 1984, and 2000.

Did you all get a copy of the handout when you came in? OK, good, so now please look at the graphs on your handout. What you'll notice immediately is that there has been a huge change in people's voting patterns over the past 40-something years. In 1964, a great majority of votes – about 90 percent – were for the Democratic candidate for President, Lyndon Johnson. Twenty years later, there was a dramatic change, and over 97 percent of the votes went to the Republican candidate, Ronald Reagan. And then 16 years later, the votes were more equally divided. In fact, the country was split down the middle – about half voted for the Republican candidate, George W. Bush, and half for the Democratic candidate, Al Gore. In the end, the Republicans won that year, but the results were very, very close.

Why do changes like these happen? How do we explain them? Well, sometimes changes in voting patterns are the result of economic conditions, meaning, for example, that voters are responding to high employment or unemployment. A strong economy helped Ronald Reagan get elected for a second term in 1984, for example. Or, there could be other reasons, such as concern about the international situation. The attack of September 11, 2001, was probably a factor in George W. Bush's reelection in 2004. But obviously, a third reason for changing voting patterns is that new generations of voters have different values from the generations that came before them. Generation Y-ers do not necessarily vote the same way as their parents, the Baby Boomers. And people's values often change as they get older.

I want to emphasize that I've been discussing American political values and the political system in a very general way. In practice, many people are not strict conservatives or liberals; they may have conservative beliefs on some issues and liberal ideas on others. And all Democrats and Republicans are not the same, either. You know, often we see our country divided on the map between red and blue states. But in my opinion, all 50 states are actually different shades of purple because there are both conservative and liberal voters in every state in the nation.

Narrator: Now complete the steps in your book.

9

Narrator: Chapter 9, American Innovations
Page 131
Listening for specific information, Step 2

Narrator: One.

Woman: The battery was invented in 1800 in Italy.

Narrator: Two.

Woman: The bar code was invented in the United States. It was first used in Ohio in 1974.

Narrator: Three.

Woman: The ballpoint pen was invented in America in 1888.

Narrator: Four.

Woman: Post-It® notes were invented in 1974 by an American.

Narrator: Five.

Woman: The microwave oven was invented in the 1940s in the United States.

Narrator: Six.

Woman: The modern ring pull was invented in 1975 by an American.

Narrator: Seven.

Woman: The Band-Aid®, an American invention, first appeared in 1920.

Narrator: Eight.

Woman: The portable workbench was invented in South Africa in 1961.

Narrator: Nine.

Woman: Reflective "cat's eyes" were invented in 1933 in Great Britain.

Narrator: Ten.

Woman: The parking meter was invented in the 1930s in the United States.

Narrator: Now complete the steps in your book.

Narrator: Chapter 9, American Innovations
Page 133
Answering multiple choice questions, Step 2

Interviewer: Hello, Cristina. I want to ask you about your experience with digital technology. Has it changed your life much?

Cristina: You mean computers, electronic gadgets, things like that?

Interviewer: Yeah.

Cristina: Well, actually, I didn't start using computers until late in my life. The first ones came out when I was already an adult, and I thought they were hard to use. You had to learn a whole new language, and for me, that was very difficult.

Interviewer: Do you use a computer now?

Cristina: Yes . . . but let me tell you an embarrassing secret. For a long time, I had no idea what e-mail meant. But when I started my last job as a college professor, some colleagues took me aside and told me, "We're going to put you in the twenty-first century." And they showed me how to use the Internet and e-mail, and of course now I use them every day, and I've become quite proficient. I especially like doing research online, because search engines help me find things very quickly. And I'm even thinking about putting my courses online in the future so that I can post links to art and sound files.

Interviewer: What other kinds of technological innovations do you use . . . I mean, in your everyday life?

Cristina: Well, recently, I upgraded to a really powerful computer, and I watch DVDs and record TV shows on it. I also got an iPod, so that I can download music from the Internet and listen to it on the train on my way to work.

Interviewer: Wow, you've become quite technological!

Cristina: Yeah, and yet . . . let me tell you, I do think all this technology has some drawbacks. I mean, my e-mail is always full of spam, and people are always bothering me with jokes and questions. And another thing I hate are cell phones. I find them very annoying and intrusive, especially when people use them in restaurants. I don't want to be in touch with everyone all the time. That's a major disadvantage of all this technology – there is no privacy anymore.

Interviewer: I know exactly what you mean. Thank you. Now Victor, you're 20, right? How important is digital technology in your life?

Victor: Extremely important. I actually can't remember life without a computer in the house. I remember very distinctly telling my parents that all I wanted for my eighth birthday was electronics. I got my first laptop when I was 11, and I've had one ever since. I use it all the time.

Interviewer: What for?

Victor: Everything! The one I have now is wireless, so I take it everywhere. Of course I use it to listen to music, and to IM my friends - but more important, I use it for college because all the readings and syllabi are online. We have discussion groups online, the professor posts our grades online and there are podcasts of many lectures, so I download them and listen to them whenever. So I'm online 24/7. Well, except when I'm sleeping, of course.

Interviewer: Do you think all this technology makes it easier to study?

Victor: Well, sometimes I'm not sure. On one hand, technology saves time, because it's so convenient. I mean, it's faster to find stuff on the Internet than go look for it in a library! And definitely the Internet gives you a lot of information that's very valuable. But I'll tell you something. I usually make outlines of my essays with a pencil and paper, because I can't always think clearly if I'm looking at a computer screen.

Interviewer: I know, I feel that way, too. Why do you think that is?

Victor: I think that's because it's uncomfortable. It's not too good for your back to be sitting at a computer all day long. And another disadvantage is that once I start talking to my friends online, I waste a lot of time.

Narrator: Now complete the steps in your book.

Narrator: Chapter 9, American Innovations
Page 135
Drawing inferences, Step 2

Interviewer: Ronnie, what kind of sports do you play?

Ronnie: Soccer. That's really my favorite sport. And I like rugby, too.

Interviewer: Do you? And do you like any sports that are more traditionally American, like . . .

Ronnie: You mean like baseball and basketball?

Interviewer: Yeah.

Ronnie: Yeah, I play those, too. I like all sports, actually. In the summer, we always get a group of guys together to play baseball in the park. But baseball is a summer game. In the winter, I play basketball.

Interviewer: And what about sports like skateboarding and Rollerblading? You know, they started in America, too, and they're really popular right now.

Ronnie: Look, everybody likes speed. When I was really small, I had a bicycle and I used to ride down the hill as fast as I could. And snowboarding is really, really fast. That's why young people like it! And plus, it's kind of trendy. It's like, "Other guys are doing it, so I want to do it, too." When I saw them snowboarding during the winter Olympics, I thought, "Wow, I really want to try that some day."

Interviewer: And do you think you will?

Ronnie: Well, I'm not sure. You have to have special equipment for snowboarding and a lot of those "extreme sports," and so even though they might be fun, they can get pretty expensive. And plus, I think most extreme sports are dangerous. A lot of people get injured doing them.

Interviewer: Thanks, Ronnie. Now, let's change the subject here and let me ask you, Mara, the U.S. has always been a big innovator in movies, and I know you like film, right?

Mara: Yeah, I love all kinds of films, even the old black and white ones. In fact, they sometimes have better stories than the modern blockbusters. But actually what I'm really interested in are all the special effects that the modern films have. I think they're so innovative. I mean that about 40 years ago, movies were only made with cameras, but today they also use computers and advanced software programs to create all kinds of visual effects.

Interviewer: Could you give me an example?

Mara: Yeah, like they can cut and paste people into scenes, like in that movie with Tom Hanks, *Forrest Gump*, where they show the main character in a scene with Richard Nixon, the president from about 30 years earlier.

Interviewer: Yes, I remember that.

Mara: And then there's computer animation . . . it's unbelievable how they can make animals and cartoon figures come to life.

Interviewer: So you like animated films?

Mara: Oh, yeah! Remember *Shrek*? They made his movements look absolutely human. And the technology is getting better and better. The only problem, as far as I can see, is that perhaps the modern movies rely too much on computers. I find that sometimes the plots and acting aren't all that good.

Narrator: Now complete the steps in your book.

Narrator: Chapter 9, American Innovations Page 139 Note taking: Listening for similarities and differences, Step 2

Narrator: One.

Daniel Erker: Like the blues, country also developed as a unique musical genre.

Narrator: Two.

Daniel Erker: The other big similarity to the blues is that country is a uniquely American genre.

Narrator: Three.

Daniel Erker: But that's where the similarities end, because of course, blues and country are very distinct.

Narrator: Four.

Daniel Erker: So country music came from a different geographic area than the blues.

Narrator: Five.

Daniel Erker: While country music traditionally had some of the same sad themes as the blues, it included positive themes, too.

Narrator: Six.

Daniel Erker: The third difference, of course, is that country sounds very different from the blues.

Narrator: Seven.

Daniel Erker: Unlike the blues, country is often played by groups of musicians and singers, not just one.

Narrator: Now complete the steps in your book.

**Narrator: Chapter 9, American Innovations
Page 140
Note taking: Choosing a format for your
notes, Step 1**

Daniel Erker: What do you think of when you hear the words *American music*? Perhaps you imagine a particular performer, or a band, or a specific musical instrument. But what I want to look at today are two uniquely American musical genres, or styles: the blues and country music. I'm going to discuss them one by one: first the blues, and then country. But I'll cover more or less the same points each time; that is, the name and origins of this musical style, its unique musical elements or characteristics, and some famous musicians who play in this style.

Narrator: Now complete the steps in your book.

**Narrator: Chapter 9, American Innovations
Page 140
Note taking: Choosing a format for your
notes, Step 2**

Daniel Erker: What do you think of when you hear the words *American music*? Perhaps you imagine a particular performer, or a band, or a specific musical instrument. But what I want to look at today are two uniquely American musical genres, or styles: the blues and country music. I'm going to discuss them one by one: first the blues, and then country. But I'll cover more or less the same points each time; that is, the name and origins of this musical style, its unique musical elements or characteristics, and some famous musicians who play in this style.

So let's begin with the blues. Where did it get its name? Most people agree that the name – blues – is connected with *having the blues*, which means that a person is feeling sad, troubled, or, you know, melancholy. This strong feeling is what allows blues musicians to create their music. The blues originated among freed African slaves and their children and grandchildren in an area of the state of Mississippi called the Delta. As a unique musical genre, we're not sure exactly when the blues first appeared, but it was actually based on the songs that slaves used to sing when they were working in the fields before the Civil War. The first recordings of blues songs were made around the beginning of the twentieth century.

Now, as I said, the blues is a unique musical genre, and by that I mean – well, the elements it includes, like the instruments, the themes, and the form. Well, originally the blues was performed by a single singer playing a guitar or a banjo. That's all. Later, other instruments such as the piano and harmonica became important, too. But most often, the blues was, and still is, played by a lone bluesman, playing the guitar and singing about lost love, poverty, and the cruelty of life, and also other basic human problems, especially the problems of slave life. As for the musical form of the blues, I'm going to play a short example for you so you can get a feeling of what a typical blues song sounds like. [*plays musical passage*]

One of the most famous blues players ever was Robert Johnson. In fact, he's been called the most important blues musician who ever lived. What is really interesting about him is that he only recorded 29 songs in his short life. He died in 1938 when he was only 26 years old, and only two photographs of him exist. If you've never heard his music, you can listen to it on the Internet and hear what real early blues music sounded like.

So over time, the blues moved into the cities and started to be popular with large numbers of people. During the twentieth century it became more commercialized, and it influenced the creation of other musical genres such as jazz, rhythm and blues, and rock 'n' roll.

Narrator: Now complete the steps in your book.

Narrator: Chapter 9, American Innovations
Page 142
Note taking: Choosing a format for your notes, Step 1

Daniel Erker: Now another original American musical genre is called country, and that's what I'll talk about next. Like the blues, country also developed as a unique musical genre, and in fact, it was influenced by early blues music as well as black church music and folk music from Britain. And of course, the other big similarity to the blues is that country is a uniquely American genre. In other words, it was born in America and is one of America's most popular musical innovations.

But that's where the similarities end, because of course, blues and country are very distinct. Country music got its name because it was played by the descendents of white European immigrants who lived in rural areas of Appalachia, specifically in the states of Tennessee, Virginia, and Kentucky. So country music came from a different geographic area than the blues.

Next, while country music traditionally had some of the same sad themes as the blues, it included positive themes, too, like the musicians' devotion to their homes and families, love of freedom and independence, and their love of the land. Many country songs have religious themes, too.

The third difference, of course, is that country sounds very different from the blues. Unlike the blues, country is often played by groups of musicians and singers, not just one. And that way you can have singers singing in harmony. Also, country music generally uses a wider variety of instruments than the blues – not only guitars and banjos, but also piano, drums, violin, bass, mandolin, and nowadays, of course, the electric guitar and electric piano, which really changed the sound. A typical country song might sound like this. [*plays musical passage*]

If we count the number of radio stations in the United States that play country music, then country is the most popular musical genre in the U.S. today. One of the most popular country musicians ever is Willie Nelson. He has been active since the 1950s and is considered a national treasure. Other famous musicians you might know are Faith Hill and the Dixie Chicks. If you're interested in exploring this topic more, all you have to do is listen to one of the hundreds of country radio stations around the country or online.

Narrator: Now complete the steps in your book.

10

Narrator: Chapter 10, Global Transformations
Page 145
Listening for tone of voice, Step 2

Narrator: One.

Woman: The first photo shows an advertisement for Kentucky Fried Chicken, right?

Man: Yeah. It was taken in Kuwait.

Woman: Are you sure?!

Narrator: Two.

Man: Let's see, this photo is of McDonalds, but . . . was it taken in Korea?

Woman: Nope, Japan. See the letters? That's Japanese.

Man: Oh, yeah . . . yeah, I see.

Narrator: Three.

Woman: OK. This looks like . . . it's a restaurant called Pollo Loco. That's Spanish.

Man: But the photo was actually taken in Los Angeles.

Woman: Oh, yeah. Of course, there are lots of Latino restaurants in L.A.

Narrator: Four.

Man: And this last photo . . . oh, this has to be an ad for Coca Cola.

Woman: Yes, but the photo was taken in Thailand.

Man: Really?! Oh, yeah! Now I see . . . the letters aren't in English.

Narrator: Now complete the steps in your book.

Narrator: Chapter 10, Global Transformations
Page 147
Retelling what you have heard, Step 2

Interviewer: You were telling me that you tried acupuncture, Adam. But I'm not sure I understand exactly what it is.

Adam: Well, you see . . . an acupuncturist puts needles into different parts of your body.

Interviewer: Doesn't it hurt?

Adam: Oh, no. The needles just go in a little way.

Interviewer: And what do the needles do?

Adam: Well, I'm not sure exactly how it works. But the idea is that if the needles are put in the right place, they can help you get over your physical problem.

Interviewer: And acupuncture worked for you.

Adam: Yeah, it did. A couple of years ago I was having a lot of headaches. I didn't want to take pain pills because they made me so sleepy, so I decided to try an alternative treatment instead. And I'd read about acupuncture, so I tried it, and it worked!

Interviewer: Is acupuncture popular among the people you know?

Adam: Well, it's becoming more and more accepted. I read somewhere that about 20 million Americans have tried it. And, well, you can understand why – after all, it goes back about 21,000 years!

Interviewer: What were its origins?

Adam: I think it started in Asia. And it's still very common throughout Asia.

Interviewer: Is it practiced differently in the United States than in Asia?

Adam: Well, I'm not sure. But people in Asian countries think of it differently than we

do. In Asia, acupuncture is considered an ancient medical practice. But in the U.S., it's become kind of a luxury because most health insurance companies don't cover it. And that's also true about other alternative treatments. But a lot of people still use them.

Interviewer: Well, a lot of people are certainly practicing yoga these days. I guess you could call yoga an example of alternative exercise. Maria, you practice yoga, don't you?

Maria: Yes, I do. I take a class at my gym every Tuesday.

Interviewer: And if there's a class at your gym, that just proves how popular yoga is nowadays.

Maria: Yeah. It's very popular now. There are yoga classes going on all around my college. My friends are all signing up to take them. I mean, you know, it's really trendy.

Interviewer: But do you like it? Or are you just taking it because it's trendy?

Maria: Oh, no, I really love it! It helps you relax your body and your mind, too. It's very cool.

Interviewer: Did you know that yoga is a traditional religious practice?

Maria: Yeah, I know that. It's originally from India. You know, I think it's part of the Hindu religion. Anyway, it's been around for over 2,000 years and there's a whole philosophy behind it. But in the classes my friends and I take . . . we just do the exercise part. I think lots of people in the U.S. think of it mainly as exercise.

Narrator: Now complete the steps in your book.

Narrator: Chapter 10, Global Transformations
Page 148
Retelling what you have heard, Step 2

Interviewer: So, let's start with you, Lindsay. You said you wanted to talk about your car.

Lindsay: Yes. It comes from Germany.

Interviewer: And what kind is it?

Lindsay: It's a Volkswagen. The reason I love it is because it's small, so it's easy to get in and out of traffic and that's important for me because I live in Miami where there're lots of people and lots of cars! And another advantage is that it's easier to park.

Interviewer: You were saying that there are often differences between German and American cars. Isn't that right?

Lindsay: Yes, because in America people like automatics. But in Germany they sell mostly cars with manual transmissions. And also I think that for the U.S. market they make a lot of cars with bigger engines.

Interviewer: Oh, really?

Lindsay: Well, that's probably because gas is cheaper in the States than in Europe.

Interviewer: OK. Now, Chander. I know you live in New York now, but you're originally from India?

Chander: That's right.

Interviewer: And you own a very popular restaurant in New York. What kind of food do you serve?

Chander: We serve authentic Indian food.

Interviewer: So it's just like eating in a restaurant in India?

Chander: Yes, but . . . sometimes we have to change the recipes a little bit.

Interviewer: Why is that?

Chander: You see, Indian food has certain spices that are quite strong. You have to try them two or three times before you get used to the taste. And some of them also taste very hot. So we don't always use them in our dishes, because they're not familiar to Americans.

Interviewer: That's interesting!

Chander: And also we don't serve quite as much rice as we would in India, because Americans tend to eat less rice. They eat more meat and vegetables.

Interviewer: But all your dishes use authentic Indian ingredients, don't they?

Chander: Well, almost all. You know, many of my American customers like a creamy taste. So sometimes the chef will put in just a little mayonnaise or sour cream. We don't

use those ingredients at all in India, but we do here!

Narrator: Now complete the steps in your book.

Narrator: Chapter 10, Global Transformations Page 153
Note taking: Listening for restatements, Step 2

Narrator: One.

Cynthia Wiseman: Slang is, and I'm quoting a dictionary here, "a type of language used especially in speech among particular speech communities" – that is, groups of people who use language in a particular way that's acceptable to all of them.

Narrator: Two.

Cynthia Wiseman: Slang is tremendously popular among young people, because it's all about what's happening now. That means that it evolves, or in other words, adapts and changes rapidly.

Narrator: Three.

Cynthia Wiseman: This way of speaking is very attractive. It's creative and cool, as I mentioned, and it's very youth-oriented, meaning that it appeals to young people.

Narrator: Four.

Cynthia Wiseman: Young people around the world hear celebrities, you know, famous actors or singers, speaking or singing American slang.

Narrator: Five.

Cynthia Wiseman: In the last quarter century, this word has invaded every corner of the English-speaking world. I mean, you hear it almost everywhere you go.

Narrator: Now complete the steps in your book.

Cynthia Wiseman: Good afternoon. Welcome, everyone. The focus of today's lecture is the globalization of American slang. In other words, how American English slang is used by people all over the world. You see, American slang has been transformed into a global form of communication, in a sense. Wherever you travel in the world today – to Turkey, to Italy, or Mexico, or Korea – you hear people using a lot of American slang. Now, as a professor of linguistics, I'm very interested in this phenomenon, so whenever I go to another country I always tape conversations with people so that I can study what they're saying. I'm going to play you some of these conversations. Now, in this first example, I was in a store in Cairo, in Egypt. Listen to my conversation.

[*plays tape*]
Cynthia: *Thank you very much for your help.*
Store owner: *No problem.*
[*stops tape*]

See what the store owner said? He didn't say, "You're welcome," he said, "No problem." He didn't learn that expression in a textbook!

Here's another example. This time, I was having a conversation with a young woman I met on the street in Poland.

[*plays tape*]
Cynthia: *This is the first time I've been to Poland.*
Young woman: *Cool.*
[*stops tape*]

Notice how the speaker didn't say "all right" or even "OK." She said, "Cool." See . . . American slang. Why is this form of speaking so popular? How does it spread across the world? In this part of the lecture I'll discuss several characteristics, or features, of slang. In the second part, we'll look at how American slang seems to travel the globe so effortlessly.

So, let's start with a definition. Slang is, and I'm quoting a dictionary here, "a type of language used especially in speech among particular speech communities" – that is, groups of people who use language in a particular way that's acceptable to all of them. And then the dictionary also says, "Slang is considered very informal." I'd like to talk about these characteristics one by one.

Number one, slang is used mostly when we are speaking, and less often in writing, especially in any formal writing. People do use slang in e-mails, it's true, but e-mail and online "chats" as we call them, are really more like spoken language. Let me give you an example. When you're speaking to someone, you often say "hi" or "hey," but those words are much less common in writing. So in general, slang is used in speech, and it's much more informal than regular English.

Second, slang is used within a particular group. In fact, if you use slang words and expressions, that shows that you are part of the same group as the person you're speaking to, whether that's a student group, a music group, or some other group. What's really interesting, though, is that even though most slang begins in a group, sometimes it becomes so popular that everyone begins to use it. That's what happened with the word *cool*, meaning "good" or "fashionable." *Cool* was first used by jazz musicians in the 1930s, but as jazz became more popular, more and more people began to use the word. We're still using it 80 years later.

Another characteristic of slang is that it's incredibly creative. Slang is tremendously popular among young people, because it's all about what's happening now. That means that it evolves, or in other words, adapts and changes rapidly, as people create new ways to respond to a situation. In the '60s, people said "groovy," meaning "good," but nowadays people say "awesome" or "sweet" to mean "good." You can use these words, but perhaps I'm a little too old to say "sweet."

Narrator: Now complete the steps in your book.

Narrator: Chapter 10, Global Transformations Page 155
Note taking: Combining the skills, Step 1

Cynthia Wiseman: Now we have to recognize that this way of speaking is very attractive. It's creative and cool, as I mentioned, and it's very youth-oriented, meaning that it appeals to young people. But there are two other factors that explain its worldwide appeal.

The first one is that American slang is spread by music, TV, and movies, which are gaining in popularity all over the world. This allows new expressions to spread among many people in a very short time. In particular, TV allows American slang to spread like wildfire. Young people around the world hear celebrities, you know, famous actors or singers, speaking or singing American slang, and they quickly adopt the same words and expressions. Let me talk to you about the word *like*. In the last quarter century, this word has invaded every corner of the English-speaking world. I mean, you hear it almost everywhere you go. One article I read said that Britney Spears was the word's number-one user! And a recent study showed that college and high school students use this word in almost every situation. Listen to the following segment, recorded among American teenagers, and tell me how many times you hear this word:

[*plays tape*]
Teenager: *My friend was like, "Come on, let's go and do something," and I was like, "Where? Like, to a movie or something?"*
[*stops tape*]

How many times did you hear the word *like*? Like, two or three times?

There's a second way American slang spreads, and that's by digital technology. You know, young people today are very electronically literate. A recent study suggested that they are using media 8½ hours a day. They are surfing the Internet, listening to digital downloads or podcasts, instant messaging, and so on, for most of their waking hours. This connectedness also allows slang to spread quickly. I think I've got time to play you one more example. I was in the Dominican Republic, and I told a store owner I would come back to the store later. Listen to the store owner's response.

[*plays tape*]
Cynthia: *I don't want to buy this yet because I don't want to carry it around all day. I'll come back later, OK?*
Store owner: *OK, whatever.*
[*stops tape*]

Did you hear what he said? Yes, uh . . . ?
Student: Whatever.
Cynthia Wiseman: Whatever, yes, that's right. That means, OK, that's fine, I don't mind. It's a great example of how American slang has spread throughout the world.

Well, we're running out of time, so let's wrap this up. As you see, American slang is popular for several reasons. It's the language of young people, making it attractive and popular. It's created and communicated through TV and movies and music, which bring it to every corner of the earth. And the Internet really reinforces the power of slang.

Narrator: Now complete the steps in your book.

Lecture Quizzes
and Quiz Answers

Name _____ Date _____

Chapter **1** LECTURE QUIZ

Answer the following questions on Parts One and Two of the Chapter 1 lecture, *The Structure of the U.S. Federal Government*. Use only your lecture notes to help you. Answer each question as fully as possible. You will receive 20 points for each complete and correct answer:

1 Explain the function of each branch of the U.S. government. (20 points)

2 What are the two parts of the legislative branch? Who are the people that form this branch? (20 points)

3 Who are the most important members of the executive branch of government? (20 points)

4 Explain the judicial branch. (20 points)

5 Explain the purpose of the system of checks and balances and give an example of how it works. (20 points)

Name _____ Date _____

Chapter **2** LECTURE QUIZ

Answer the following questions on Parts One and Two of the Chapter 2 lecture, *The First Amendment*. Use only your lecture notes to help you. Answer each question as fully as possible. You will receive 20 points for each complete and correct answer:

1 Explain what freedom of religion means to Americans. (20 points)

2 What does the principle of freedom of speech mean in practice? (20 points)

3 Give two examples of freedom of the press. (20 points)

4 What two other forms of freedom are guaranteed under the First Amendment? (20 points)

5 Give three examples of controversies under the First Amendment (20 points)

Chapter 3 LECTURE QUIZ

Answer the following questions on Parts One and Two of the Chapter 3 lecture, *Immigrants to America Face Prejudice but Make Lasting Contributions*. Use only your lecture notes to help you. Answer each question as fully as possible. You will receive 20 points for each complete and correct answer:

1 What were some of the major groups that immigrated to the United States from about 1840 to 1917? (20 points)

2 In what ways did these immigrants face prejudice? (20 points)

3 What were some of the reasons for the prejudice these immigrant groups faced? (20 points)

4 The United States needed a lot of workers at this time in its history. Why? (20 points)

5 What are some of the contributions that these immigrant groups made to the United States? (20 points)

Chapter 4 LECTURE QUIZ

Answer the following questions on Parts One and Two of the Chapter 4 lecture, *Recent Immigrants and Today's United States*. Use only your lecture notes to help you. Answer each question as fully as possible. You will receive 20 points for each complete and correct answer:

1 What is a metaphor, and why do historians and writers use metaphors to describe American culture and society? (20 points)

2 What is the oldest metaphor? What is the problem with this metaphor? (20 points)

3 What other metaphors does the lecturer mention? Which is her favorite metaphor and why? (20 points)

4 Explain the meaning of *transnationalism* and give examples of this phenomenon. (20 points)

5 What are some factors that help today's immigrants keep a closer relationship with their home countries than could immigrants in the past? (20 points)

Chapter 5 LECTURE QUIZ

Answer the following questions on Parts One and Two of the Chapter 5 lecture, *The Civil Rights Movement and the Women's Movement*. Use only your lecture notes to help you. Answer each question as fully as possible. You will receive 20 points for each complete and correct answer:

1 Why was the decade of the '60s important? (20 points)

2 What was the civil rights movement, and how did it start? (20 points)

3 What were some achievements of the civil rights movement? (20 points)

4 What was the experience of many women during World War II, and what effect did that experience have? (20 points)

5 Describe women's protests in the mid-1960s and explain their successes. (20 points)

Chapter 6 LECTURE QUIZ

Answer the following questions on Parts One and Two of the Chapter 6 lecture, *Two Important Laws in the Struggle for Equality*. Use only your lecture notes to help you. Answer each question as fully as possible. You will receive 20 points for each complete and correct answer:

1 Why did the United States need the Age Discrimination Act? (20 points)

2 What does the Age Discrimination Act do, and is this law effective? (20 points)

3 What is the Americans with Disabilities Act, and when was it passed? (20 points)

4 Give some examples of the impact of the Americans with Disabilities Act. (20 points)

5 Explain President George H.W. Bush's comment, "Let the shameful wall of exclusion come tumbling down." (20 points)

Chapter **7** LECTURE QUIZ

Answer the following questions on Parts One and Two of the Chapter 7 lecture, *Three American Folk Heroes*. Use only your lecture notes to help you. Answer each question as fully as possible. You will receive 20 points for each complete and correct answer:

1 Why does the lecturer discuss the cowboy, the entrepreneur, and the superhero? (20 points)

2 Why is the cowboy such a popular image in U.S. culture? How does the lecturer illustrate the cowboy's attraction? (20 points)

3 What values does the entrepreneur represent? What are some examples of entrepreneurs? (20 points)

4 When did the superhero image become popular, and what values do superheroes represent? (20 points)

5 Explain the lecturer's response to the question about women folk heroes. (20 points)

Chapter **8** LECTURE QUIZ

Answer the following questions on Parts One and Two of the Chapter 8 lecture, *Conservative and Liberal Values in American Politics*. Use only your lecture notes to help you. Answer each question as fully as possible. You will receive 20 points for each complete and correct answer:

1 Why does the lecturer emphasize the fact that we must discuss conservative and liberal values in a general way? (20 points)

2 How do conservatives and liberals generally see the role of the government? (20 points)

3 How do conservatives and liberals often disagree about taxes? (20 points)

4 Describe conservative and liberal views on business. (20 points)

5 Why do voting patterns often change so dramatically? (20 points)

Chapter **9** LECTURE QUIZ

Answer the following questions on Parts One and Two of the Chapter 9 lecture, *The Blues and Country Music: Two American Musical Genres*. Use only your lecture notes to help you. Answer each question as fully as possible. You will receive 20 points for each complete and correct answer:

1 What are the main points of comparison the lecturer makes between the blues and country music? (20 points)

2 When and where did the blues originate? (20 points)

3 Name a famous blues player and the instruments and themes that the blues often includes. (20 points)

4 In what ways is country music similar to the blues? (20 points)

5 Explain some ways that country music is different from the blues. (20 points)

Chapter 10 LECTURE QUIZ

Answer the following questions on Parts One and Two of the Chapter 10 lecture, *The Globalization of American Slang*. Use only your lecture notes to help you. Answer each question as fully as possible. You will receive 20 points for each complete and correct answer:

1 Explain what the lecturer means when she says that "American slang has been transformed into a global form of communication." (20 points)

2 What are three characteristics of slang, according to the lecturer? (20 points)

3 Give several examples of the slang expressions, past and present, that the lecturer points out. (20 points)

4 How does the media help to spread American slang? (20 points)

5 What is the second way that American slang spreads all over the world? (20 points)

Lecture Quiz Answers

Chapter **1** LECTURE QUIZ ANSWERS

1 The legislative branch (Congress) makes the laws. The executive branch approves the laws that Congress makes. The judicial branch interprets the laws that Congress passes. In other words, its members decide if a law is constitutional or not.

2 The two parts of the legislative branch are the Senate and the House of Representatives. There are two Senators from each state, for a total of 100 senators. The number of representatives depends on the size of each state's population.

3 The most important people are the President, the Vice President, and the heads of government departments, who are called secretaries (Secretary of State, Secretary of Defense, Secretary of Education, and so on).

4 The judicial branch of the federal government is the Supreme Court, which is the highest court in the land. It has nine members, called justices. These justices decide whether laws or other court decisions are constitutional.

5 The system of checks and balances ensures that no one person or branch of the government has too much power. The three branches have the power to check, or limit, each other's actions. One example is that although the Supreme Court justices are chosen by the President, the Senate has the power to approve or deny the President's choice.

Chapter **2** LECTURE QUIZ ANSWERS

1 Freedom of religion means that Americans are free to practice their religion without interference from the government and that there is no national religion.

2 In practice, freedom of speech means being able to talk openly about your ideas, even if other people disagree with them. Americans also have the freedom to read or listen to others' ideas. Freedom of speech also includes "symbolic" speech, including pictures, music, and fashion.

3 The press can criticize the government and even make fun of government leaders. Journalists have the right to oppose the government's actions in print.

4 The other two forms of freedom are freedom of assembly, which is the right to meet in groups, and freedom of petition, which means citizens have the right to ask the government to change laws or policies.

5 Flag burning, cell phones in school, and prayers in public school are three examples of controversies under the First Amendment.

Chapter **3** LECTURE QUIZ ANSWERS

1 The major immigrant groups were the Germans, Irish, Jews from Russia, and Italians, as well as people from Poland, Greece, Hungary, China, and Mexico.

2 These immigrant groups were refused apartments, refused jobs, and called cruel names.

3 Many Americans were frightened about the size and diversity of the new foreign population. Immigrants also faced prejudice because of their different religious beliefs, languages, and customs. Americans were afraid that they did not share the country's democratic values. Some people were also afraid that they would lose their jobs as a result of immigrant labor.

4 The United States needed a lot of workers because it was a time of great expansion. Cities and industries were growing, and a lot of people were moving west.

5 These immigrant groups became farmers, tailors, bakers, and butchers. They helped build the infrastructure of many American cities. They were also active in culture and education.

Chapter **4** LECTURE QUIZ ANSWERS

1 A metaphor is an image or model that is used to help us understand things that are complex, like America's diverse and complex society and culture.

2 The oldest metaphor is the melting pot, in which different ingredients mix together to make something new. The problem with this metaphor is that it doesn't always describe today's reality, in which many immigrants do not completely assimilate to mainstream society.

3 Other metaphors are the salad bowl, the patchwork quilt, and the kaleidoscope. The lecturer's favorite metaphor is the kaleidoscope, which shows America as a colorful picture of a multiracial, multiethnic, multicultural society that is always changing.

4 *Transnationalism* describes a person's experience across nations or cultures or their continuing relationship with their home countries. For example, many immigrants own homes or businesses in their country of origin, send money to family members in their home country, or stay involved in business or political affairs there.

5 Ease of travel and technology are two factors that help today's immigrants keep a closer relationship with their home countries than immigrants in the past could.

Chapter 5 LECTURE QUIZ ANSWERS

1 The '60s was a time of great and often violent change in the United States. During this decade, there were many political and social movements, such as the movement against the war in Vietnam, the civil rights movement, and the women's movement.

2 The civil rights movement was the struggle by hundreds of thousands of people working to achieve equal rights for African Americans. It started because almost 100 years after the end of slavery in the United States, segregation and discrimination against blacks was still common.

3 As a result of the civil rights movement, the Jim Crow laws were overturned, and the federal government passed laws that guaranteed the rights of black Americans. Other groups also started fighting for justice and equality.

4 During World War II, many women took over men's jobs while they were fighting in Europe and Asia. When the men returned from the war and to their jobs, women felt dissatisfied with returning to their roles as wives and mothers.

5 In the mid-1960s, women marched in the streets, tried to elect more women to Congress, and demanded equal opportunities for women in education and at work. Today, "equal pay for equal work" is the law. More women than men go to college, and there are women politicians and university presidents.

Chapter 6 LECTURE QUIZ ANSWERS

1 Before the Age Discrimination Act was passed, older people faced a lot of discrimination in the workplace. For example, employers could set an age limit for job applicants.

2 The Act protects people over 40 years old from discrimination at work in areas such as hiring and firing, benefits, and retirement. However, there are still many legal complaints about age discrimination.

3 The Americans with Disabilities Act was passed in 1990 to protect people with disabilities from discrimination.

4 The Americans with Disabilities Act has improved life for thousands of disabled people in the areas of public transportation, access to buildings and other public spaces, and hiring and education practices.

5 This comment means that our goal should be inclusion, meaning equality and full participation for all people, including people with disabilities.

Chapter 7 LECTURE QUIZ ANSWERS

1 The cowboy, the entrepreneur, and the superhero are images that most Americans know about from traditional songs, stories, or actual history. These images surround us in advertising and daily culture.

2 The cowboy represents courage, freedom, and independence, an image that became popular in the nineteenth century when people moved west to make their fortune. The lecturer describes the cowboy's attraction as representing some core American values: courage, freedom, and independence. He points out that most of the students are wearing jeans.

3 The entrepreneur represents the idea that if you are smart, have good ideas, and work hard, you can succeed. Examples include Andrew Carnegie, who made millions of dollars from steel factories, and John D. Rockefeller, who made his fortune in oil.

4 The superhero became popular in the 1930s. Superheroes are symbols of justice and law.

5 The lecturer says that most traditional folk heroes were men but mentions Annie Oakley and Wonder Woman as examples of real and imaginary women folk heroes. He believes that there will be more women folk heroes in the future.

Chapter 8 LECTURE QUIZ ANSWERS

1 The lecturer points out that it is hard to make specific statements about Americans' political views because of the size and diversity of the population.

2 Conservatives tend to put more emphasis on personal responsibility than on government responsibility for social programs. Liberals believe in greater government responsibility.

3 Conservatives usually think government is too big and expensive, requiring high taxes, whereas liberals tend to think taxes are necessary to support social programs.

4 Conservatives typically support an economy without government control, whereas liberals think business should be closely regulated.

5 Changes in voting patterns can be the result of satisfaction or dissatisfaction with economic conditions or the international situation or differences in attitude between different generations of voters.

Chapter 9 LECTURE QUIZ ANSWERS

1 The lecturer compares the blues and country music in terms of their name and origins, unique musical elements, and famous musicians.

2 The blues originated among freed African slaves and their children and grandchildren in the Mississippi Delta before the Civil War.

3 The blues traditionally included a single singer playing a guitar or banjo, singing about lost love, poverty, the cruelty of life, and other problems. One of the most famous blues musicians was Robert Johnson.

4 Like the blues, country music developed as a uniquely American musical genre and was influenced by the blues as well as by black church music and folk music from Britain.

5 Country music was traditionally played by the descendants of white European immigrants in Appalachia. It includes a greater variety of themes and instruments and has a different musical structure.

Chapter 10 LECTURE QUIZ ANSWERS

1 The lecturer points out that wherever you travel in the world today, you hear people using American slang.

2 Slang is used mostly in speaking, rather than writing; it is used within a particular group; and it is changeable and creative.

3 The lecturer comments on the words and expressions *no problem*, *cool*, *hi*, *hey*, *groovy*, *awesome*, *sweet*, *like*, and *whatever*.

4 American TV, music, and movies, which are popular all over the world, allow young people to hear celebrities speaking or singing American slang.

5 Slang also spreads via the Internet and other electronic media, which young people may be using most of their waking hours.

Notes